60

BLESSED DECLARATIONS

BOLA OYEDELE

"You will also declare a thing,

And it will be established for you;

So light will shine on your ways."

Job 22:28

CONTENT

Dedication

Acknowledgements

Testimonies

Introduction   1

Chapter One   -   Blessed Declarations   5

Chapter Two   -   Mothers Declarations   81

Chapter Three -   Warfare Declarations   115

DEDICATION

To Jehovah God who separated me from my mother's womb and called me into His service. Thank you, Lord, for calling me, and equipping me for the work of service. I am grateful and humbled to be called a Woman of God, and for preserving my life on earth unto 60 years.

"But you are a chosen generation, a royal priesthood, a holy nation, His own special people, that you may proclaim the praises of Him who called you out of darkness into His marvellous light; who once were not a people but are now the people of God, who had not obtained mercy but now have obtained mercy."
(1 Peter 2:9-10)

ACKNOWLEDGEMENTS

My utmost gratitude is to the Almighty God for His grace and empowerment that sustained me throughout my Christian journey till the age of 60. I thank you, Lord, for all the victories and breakthroughs that continue to enforce my dominion for all the key assignments entrusted to me.

I give thanks to my spiritual father Apostle Jones Boateng for taking me from my broken state in January 2009, wiped away my tears, stilled the raging storms, taught me deliverance, patiently mentored me to become a deliverance minister, and to take my place in destiny. Papa, you gave me room to grow in DOM Church, working with you to serve the people of God, and especially in leading the Women. I thank your wife Mama Beryl Jones Boateng, together you gave me room, space and place to keep on serving. It is out of my dedicated service to the women under your tutelage, that this book has been produced. By the grace of God I will continue to serve with you in the Kingdom until Christ returns. May your horns continue to be exalted like a unicorn and the Oil on your head overflow, in Jesus name.

Many thanks to all the Pastors, Elders, Workers, Members, Children and Youths; at Deliverance Outreach Ministry (DOM) for your love, support, encouragement, and prayers all these years.

My gratitude also goes to all DOM women and other Women connected to the Church, whom I have been opportune to serve since August 2009. Thank you all for your support and encouragement in my leadership role; May the Lord honour and surround you all with Favour as a shield, as we continue to build, grow and serve together, in Jesus' name.

My profound appreciation goes to Minister Yinka Adeduntan and Sister Caroline Otim, who compiled the raw scripts of this book. Most importantly, they have assisted me to serve effectively by transmitting all women's prayer points from 2012 to 2020; and monthly declarations to all women within and outside the Church from 2011 till date, and this will continue till Christ returns, in Jesus name. I thank Elder Jane Morrison, Elder Agatha Mwaluseke, Minister Vivian Lamptey, Minister Lorraine Oliver, Sister Marion Barrett and Rachael Oyedele, for all your precious time in editing this book. May the Lord continue to strengthen and endow you all with power for manifestation, of the declaration of those things which are most surely believed among us, (Luke 1:1), in Jesus name.

I sincerely thank my siblings, children and grandchildren for all your care, patience, understanding, and assistance in various ways, as I commit to demands and sacrifices of my Kingdom assignment. I love you all dearly, and pray for God's love to keep us in the bond of peace and unity in Jesus name.

TESTIMONIES

Yinka Adeduntan

I was introduced to Pastor Bola Oyedele as the Women Pastor at Deliverance Outreach Ministries DOM) for the first time in January 2012 and very quickly, I realised that Pastor Bola has a profound passion to see Women spiritually built up in God and delivered from the shackles and afflictions of the devil on ourselves and our families. Pastor Bola's passion for women is what drew me to begin supporting and assisting her work from 2012 to 2017 as her Administrator, I produced documents, I shared phenomenal prayer points with declarations and other materials to women in the UK and worldwide, assisting with introducing new women to DOM's Women ministry, etc. To be candid, the monthly prayer points and declarations were and still are great tools that helped me in the midnight hour and there were many!

I am grateful to God for Pastor Bola for many, many reasons, for example, when I was still new at DOM and to deliverance, she really encouraged me to attend all the services, counselling sessions, etc and to learn from our Senior Pastor, Apostle Jones Dada Boateng's deliverance teachings, and how to pray deliverance prayers, she even helped me to select from the many books of our Senior Pastor which have helped me to become an ever-growing Prayer Warrior till today.

Another passion of Pastor Bola is her charity for young women and mature women called Ruth Generation

Foundation founded 2013. It registered with me because as I grew up, there was no organisation like Ruth Generation to go to for support, and I have and still support Pastor Bola in different capacities till today; and by the grace of God I am proud to say, I am one of her many Mentees!

I have and still support Pastor Bola in her other passion for the next generation i.e. Children and Youth, which is a passion of mine, too because of the alarming rise of senseless killings of Black children and youth in London. In Feb 2017, she started the Mothers-On-The-Streets Movement with the main aim to stop knife and gun crimes among children and youth through prayer walks and supporting affected parents in the Black Communities.

Pastor Bola is also a seasoned Author like her spiritual Father Apostle Jones Dada Boateng, through her books I learnt a lot about deliverance from a woman's perspective. These are 'Mighty in Battle', 'From Barrenness to Fruitfulness', 'Spiritual Warfare with the Blood of Jesus' (my personal favourite) and 'Woman Trim your Lamp'.

Finally, I thank God Almighty for the day He brought Pastor Bola into my life, she has been strong source of encouragement, source of wisdom in deliverance to me and my family since 2012. I also thank God for adding her 60th year to her and I look forward to what more God will do through and for her in the decades to come in Jesus' name, Amen. Happy Glorious 60th Birthday, my dear beautiful and amazing Mentor, Pastor B!

Caroline Otim

First, I thank God for the life of my Spiritual father Apostle Dr Jones Dada Boateng, Head Pastor of Deliverance Outreach Ministries (DOM) Church who welcomed me in 2017. Pastor Sarah Bola Oyedele is a Pastor at DOM and Head of the Women's Ministry. I have had the privilege of working for this wonderful Woman of God since 2017 as her Assistant. She has been an inspiration to me. My role at DOM is to circulate monthly emails to our Women's Group and these include Prayer Points and Declarations and forthcoming events. I also work as an Usher at the Church. The Prayer Points and Declarations are an excellent source of encouragement and empowerment for Women and their families. It has helped me in my Spiritual Walk and faith journey. It has blessed not only me, the Women's Group worldwide but also blessed family and friends. It has taught me to never give up or give in to issues of life but fight it with confidence. You have a weapon which is the word of God use it and never fear for he is always with us, ready and waiting to hear our cry.

Thank you, Pastor Sarah Bola Oyedele, for giving me this opportunity to work with you. May God continue to bless you and your family.

INTRODUCTION

All glory to the Most High God who sustained my life to 60 years on planet earth. He has enabled me to work in His vineyard for several years, and I have seen God search my heart and promoted me from stage to stage for service in the Kingdom.

I am overwhelmed; looking back at what God has used me to pour into my generation all these years, through the gift of writing He endowed me with. From day one of coming to the Lord in October 1993, I have started writing. I published my first book in August 1994, second book in 2004, third and fourth book in 2013, fifth book in 2022 and now the sixth book to celebrate my 60th in 2024.

The essence of my celebration is to showcase the God who took me from nobody to somebody being reckoned with, to the world He and Him alone created. He took me and worked on me, both to do His Will and to do His good pleasure (Philippians 2:13).

This book is a testimony of God's work through me, as I serve patiently over the years of which I never knew I could go this far at age 60. There is an urge to do much more for His service, than where I am today; however, as I live daily in His love, mercy and faithfulness, God patiently fills me with the measure of grace, strength and power by His Spirit in my inner man, to move and carry out my unique assignments.

I am grateful to have served under my Papa, Apostle Jones for 15 and half years, as this is a period that recorded remarkable growth and turnaround in all areas of my life.

Serving the women in humility and following patiently enabled me to release every month some of the declarations you will be reading in this book. Declaration is prayer in all ramifications, but exercised as speaking your desires anytime, anywhere, anyhow, anyway that suits you.

Declaring the Word of God is the most significant means to get your voice heard both in the spirit realm and the physical world. As we live in the world of today, where multitude of voices are speaking into us, both negative and positive, the good, the bad, the ugly voices, all rising to steal, to kill and destroy our innocence. We must consciously silence them, and take control of the voices that remain are influencing our minds positively.

We have heard severally that "life does not give you what you deserve; life gives you what you demand". The best way to make demand and to be reckoned with in this world is to get your voice heard. Focusing on declarations in this book is a pronounced way to achieve this. Take them daily as doses consistently and watch a significant turnaround and transformation occur, in various areas of your spiritual, physical, emotional, and especially family life.

Although the declarations states months or dates, do understand that irrespective of this, words are spirit and they are life, as you speak prophetically you can adapt it to any situation, circumstance and condition.

Chapter two is a chapter for mothers to engage the declarations to turn situations around in their children's lives, home and spiritual life.

The essence of our living is our spirituality! Engage these declarations and you will strengthen your spirit man, your soul and mind, to bring forth right decisions, actions, good character and behaviour required for your freedom leading to a prosperous life, in Jesus name.

Thank you for celebrating my 60 years, every moment you engage these declarations.

Chapter One

BLESSED DECLARATIONS (BD)

BD No.1:

All Glory, All Honour, All Power and Praise be unto our God whose faithfulness, mercy and love endures forever.

We thank God for this month of new beginnings and double portion, for which great testimonies are already rolling in.

I stand with you to declare, that this is your time and season for a turnaround situation and you will experience a double portion of blessings in all you "lay your hands to do", throughout this year in Jesus name.

I prophesy to you and your family, that you will see the goodness of the Lord in the land of the living, you will manifest the treasures, virtues, potentials, talents and gifts in you because you are destined to WIN and destined for GREATNESS in Jesus name.

Read and Meditate on: Psalm 71:21; Psalm 112:1-3; 84:11; Psalm 18:32-33; Isaiah 58:11; Isaiah 60:10-11,15-18.

BD No 2: Prayer For The Nation

These prayer points were inspired by the killing of an innocent man by the police in August 2011 at Tottenham in London. This sparked youth's to riot across London that week.

We must arise to pray for the nation according to Proverbs 14:34 which says, "Righteousness exalts a nation, but sin is a reproach to the people".

1. We stand on 2 Chronicles 7:14 to cry for mercy over our nation, for all we have witnessed in London since the killing on Saturday which lead to riots all over London.
2. We plead the Blood of Jesus on the land, and declare Psalm 24:1 that this nation is the Lord's and the fullness thereof.
3. May God turn our leaders' hearts to fear Him; May they fall down before the Lord and the nation to serve Him. (Ps 72:11).
4. Oh Lord, establish your dominion in this nation and cause your enemies to lick the dust. (Ps 72:8-9);
5. Let every covenant with death and hell be broken in this nation (Isa 28:18).
6. Let those who walk in darkness see the light and let your light shine on those in the shadow of darkness (Isa 9:2).

7. Oh lord, execute justice for the oppressed and let the poor and needy of the nation be delivered (Psalm 103:6).

8. We pray for the healing waters to flow into this nation (Rev 22:1-2):

    i) to heal our land completely Lord;
    ii) to heal all souls affected by the rioting and looting;
    iii) to heal and rescue the souls of rioters, looters from destruction;
    iv) to heal and rebuild the ruined places;
    v) to heal and restore the streets in the cities we dwell.

9. We declare that peace, protection and the blessing of God shall reign in this nation in Jesus name. (Ezekiel 34:25-28).

God bless you as you pray in intercession.

BD No 3:

We give God all the glory for guiding us into the month of Grace. May the Lord's abundant grace continue to abound more and more for you daily, in Jesus name.

Be encouraged to stand strong in the Lord, and in the power of His might. Keep enforcing the victory won on the Cross against the enemy assigned to frustrate, weaken or stop you from possessing your possessions (Obadiah 1:17).

I decree that what God has purposed for your life will be established in this season, in Jesus name. You will surely give birth to your visions, good dreams and great ideas in this season, in Jesus name. The Lord will cause you to laugh and rejoice in this season because His mighty power has changed the order in your life, from dry seasons to productive and fruitful seasons, in Jesus name.

Read and Meditate on: Ezekiel 12:25, Isaiah 58:11, Psalm 18:32-33 and Psalm126:1-3

You are a winner destined for greatness!

BD No 4:

We thank God for the awesome move of His Power at our Women's Conference.

Women, remain confident and strong in the Lord. Keep up with the spirit of the conference as you are now endowed with Power, to go forth and manifest HIS Glory, Favour, Blessings, Wisdom and Honour.

I declare that you are a treasure in earthen vessels, and this is the set time and season for you to manifest the virtues, potentials, gifts, talents, goodness and glorious destiny in you and your families, In Jesus name.

I declare that this season will not pass you by; you will surely give birth to your visions, good dreams, great ideas and divine purpose, In Jesus name.

The Anointing to establish your special favour in this season is upon you now, RECEIVE IT, in Jesus name. Amen

Read and Meditate on: 2 Corinth 4: 7-10, 16-18; Psalm 92:10; 89:20-24; Psalm 18:32-33,50; Psalm 23:5; Psalm 110:2; 71:21; Psalm 126:1-3; Job 29:6, Isaiah 60:10-11; 15:18; Ezekiel 34:25-28 and Deut 33:26-29.

BD No 5:

We give Glory to God, for His goodness and mercy endures forever, and for ushering us into the 2nd half of the year.

The Lord has granted us this month of July as a period of *Release and Total Rest* on Every Side in all areas of our lives, in Jesus name.

I prophesy to you that, as God gave Britain victory through Andy Murray on 7/7/13, to rewrite a failed record of no wins for British Tennis players in the last 77 years; So I declare you are released into the greatest victory ever that will also cause a turnaround in your family, work, business and ministry, in Jesus name.

The Unchanging Changer, the Re-writer of destinies, is working on the treasures, virtues, potentials, talents and gifts in you; which will announce you to your generation, and you will have total rest on every side, in Jesus name.

The anointing to establish this Prophesy in this season is on you now, RECEIVE IT! RECEIVE IT! RECEIVE IT! In Jesus Mighty Name.

Read and Meditate on: Psalm 126: 1-3; Psalm 18:32-33, Job 29:6; Isaiah 58:11; 60:10-11, 15-18; Psalm 92:10, 89: 20-24; 23:5.

BD No 6:

Greetings in the Wonderful name of our Lord Jesus Christ.

We ascribe to God All Praises, All Worship, All Glory, All Honour and All Power, for His goodness, mercy, grace and love endures forever.

We thank God for this month of Favour and Manifestation. I declare this is your time and season for the manifestation and fulfilment of your plans and divine purposes. In the remaining months of the year, you will surely be favoured in all your endeavours and you will see the goodness of the Lord in the land of the living, In Jesus name.

I want you to believe that no matter the challenges or trials you see today, you are DESTINED to WIN and DESTINED for GREATNESS.

Ensure you continue to strengthen your relationship with God by following His Word, Principles and Promises (Joshua 1:8). Remember, the just shall live by faith, not by what we see, hear or feel, but by God's Word, God's programme and God's plan for us on the earth.

You and I will only overcome on earth by the "Triumph of our Faith" (1John 4:4).

I prophesy to you that no matter the song your enemies are singing, you will triumph over them and their wickedness. I declare that the wicked acts of wicked men is cancelled, aborted, terminated and reversed to sender, in Jesus name (Psalm 7:9-16).

This is your set time of favour: move in it, claim it, and watch it turn your expectations into manifestations.

Read and Meditate on: Psalm 102:13; Psalm 5:12; Esther 2:15; Job 10:12; Psalm 71:21; Luke 2:52; Psalm 90:17; Deuteronomy 33:23; Isaiah 60:10-11,15-18.

BD No 7:

We thank God for His goodness and mercies since the beginning of the year.

I prophesy October will be the Month of:

> O - open Doors
> C - celebration of Testimonies
> T - triumphs and Jubilation
> O - opportunities Unlimited
> B - blessing Explosion
> E - everlasting Joy
> R - restoration of Fruitfulness.

By the power of the Altar of God in you, all of the above will manifest in all areas of your life, in Jesus name.

Strongly believe that when the grace of God finds you, it will turn around your situation for good (Romans 8:28).

It will move you from:

- rejection to acceptance,

- disgrace to grace,

- shame to honour,

- lack to abundance,

- a desert land to greener pastures.

The enemies that are mocking you, will see the difference, and God will shut them up forever!

Grace will work to launch you into greatness, receive the blessings by faith and by force. In The Mighty Name of Jesus.

Read and Meditate on: Psalm107:15-16; Psalm 84:11; Isaiah 61:7; Psalm102:13; Esther 2:17; Genesis 28:3-4; Rev 3:7-8. Isaiah 45:1-3.

BD No 8:

Glory be to the Almighty God for bringing us through to November month. The Anointing of God's Grace and Blessings, will manifest in all areas of your life, in Jesus name.

Deuteronomy 1:3-11 is clear evidence of what God is communicating to you in this time and season, for you to move forward, to possess now and beyond this year.

Our God is the same yesterday, today and forever. As He spoke through Moses to the Israelites on the 1st day of the 11th month in that year, So I prophesy to you that the satanic kings that caused you to be stagnated all these years, shall be destroyed and the arm of Pharaoh is broken, in Jesus name.

Arise and take your journey, make strategic moves to possess your possessions, to reap 1,000 times manifold blessings according to the promise of The Lord in Deut 1:11, in Jesus name.

No matter what the situation looks like now, whatever the picture of impossibility you see, hear or feel; arise and move with daring faith, take drastic actions, do something new, and see the God of possibility turn your story into glory, in Jesus name.

BD No 9:

We give glory to God for His goodness, guidance and protection all through the year. I pray that you will finish this year strong, empowered and blessed to run and fly higher in the New Year, in Jesus name.

I prophesy, that you will see the manifestation of blessings and upliftment in the New Year and beyond. Your enemies may think they have succeeded in making you an eunuch or crippled you as an eagle from flying, but I speak to you that you are coming out, in Jesus name. Believe and know that only the report of The Lord, and His promises that will stand in your life.

You have been set free and destined to win in this life, because God's thoughts for you are thoughts of peace and not of evil to give you an expected end, in Jesus name.

Read and Meditate on: Jeremiah 29:11; Deut 32:11-13; Habakkuk 3:17-19; Psalm 84:11; 46:1-5; 71:21; Isaiah 40:29-31; 60:10-12; 61:7; 54:2-3;

BD No 10: Prayer for last day of the Year

We pray on this last day of the year:

- The Joy of The Lord will be your Strength to the end;

- Double Supernatural Strength awaits you to ride on the Wings of the Altar of God throughout the New Year, In Jesus name.

- You will live all your days pleasing God and walking in the spirit, doing the will of God that brings abundant blessing always, In Jesus name.

- You will be a shining light, the light of power in your home, family, community and nations, In Jesus name.

- You will dip your feet in oil; your shoes shall be iron and brass, and you shall be strong all your days, In Jesus name.

- The Lord will guide you continually, ordering your footsteps all through the year, in Jesus name.

- The gates of divine acceptance and doors of divine elevation will automatically open for you, In Jesus name.

BD No 11:

May The Lord continue to crown the year with His goodness and cause your paths to drip with abundance, in Jesus name.

We thank the great and mighty God for this prophetic month and continue to speak Double grace, Double honour, Double portion, Double restoration, Double strength, Double perfection and Double blessings into manifestation in all areas of your life, in Jesus name.

As you continue to pursue your plans, programmes, projects, proposals and potentials to achieve your vision:-

I prophesy you will overflow with double blessings for accomplishment in Jesus name. No matter the challenges or obstacles, do not give up, Persist, Persevere and Proclaim the Word of God to enforce your victory and create your world.

God said:

> *"I know you by name, and you have also found favour in my sight. My presence will go with you, and I will give you rest. This very thing that you have spoken I will do, for you have found favour in my sight, and I know you by name." (Exodus 33:12, 14, 17).*

Read and Meditate on: 1John 4:4; Jeremiah 29:11; Proverbs 23:18; Psalms 65:11.

BD No 12:

We worship and exalt the Almighty God for this month of March. I pray prophetically that the Power of Trinity, Unity, and 3rd Day of Resurrection, will manifest wonderfully in all areas of your life, in Jesus name.

As you continue your journey through the year, I declare supernatural visitation of open heavens will locate you and establish all your ordained blessings; Of glory, riches, wisdom, strength, honour, fruitfulness, increase, abundance and fulfilment in your marital destiny, financial destiny and divine health, in Jesus name.

Be BOLD, Be STRONG, Be FOCUSSED to possess them by fire, by force. No matter the challenges or obstacles, remember the Resurrection power is working in you to quicken your mortal bodies, to raise and turn them into stepping stones for your relocation, upliftment and testimonies, in Jesus name.

Read and Meditate on: Romans 8:2,11,28; Ephesians 3:20; 1John 4:4; 5:4; Jeremiah 29:11; Psalms 65:11; 67:5-7; 102:13; 90:17; 84:11; 46:4-5; Galatians 5:1; 6:8-10.

BD No 13:

We thank the great and mighty God for the month of April. May the resounding victory of our Lord Jesus Christ, won on the Cross of Calvary, be made manifest in all areas of your life, in Jesus name.

I declare supernatural release for achievements of all your plans, projects, programmes and proposals from this month henceforth, In Jesus name.

Whatever has been frustrating your efforts from achieving is cursed to die, in Jesus name.

The Anointing of God is bringing all your travails and toiling to an end, in Jesus name.

As the fourth angel in the fire delivered Shadrach, Meshach and Abednego, so I declare your release from impossibility to possibilities; failure to success; lack and insufficiency to abundance; barrenness to fruitfulness; shame and disgrace to double honour; opposition to opportunities; frustration to fulfilment in all areas of your life, in Jesus name.

Remember to keep speaking, believing and obeying: Revelation 8:3; 12:16; Daniel 3:28-29; Isaiah 45:1-3; Ephesians 3:20; Jeremiah 29:11; Psalms 65:11; 102:13; 90:17; 84:11; 46:4-5; Galatians 5:1; Hosea 2:21-22.

BD No 14:

We give glory to God for this month of May, the month of Grace to establish good patterns of the Altar of God in all areas of your life, in Jesus name. May God's grace continue to be sufficient for you throughout your journey this year; and it will make you perfect, establish, strengthen and settle you (1 Peter 5:10), in Jesus name.

I prophesy that your Grace will not leak out, it will be sufficient for you always.

You will be positioned for Grace to fulfil all your plans, projects, programmes and proposals, now and forever.

As a Daughter of Zion, your Grace will not turn to disgrace, you will be a graced Daughter, Sister, Mother, Wife, Woman of Substance, in Jesus name.

No matter the weakness, challenge, oppression, depression or defeat you face; I command a turnaround situation now in your life; I release abundant grace, strength and favour to envelope your life and family, in Jesus name.

I decree a turnaround from weakness to strength; grief to comfort; oppression to liberty; misery to joy; defeat to victory for you now, in Jesus name.

Remember to keep speaking, believing and obeying: 1Peter 5:10; 2Corinth 12:9-10; Psalm 103:6; Psalm 146:5-9; Psalm 90:17; Psalm 102:13; Psalm 84:11; Psalm 65.11; Psalm

46:4-5; Galatians 5:1; Revelation 12:14-16; Ephesians 3:20; Jeremiah 29:11.

BD No 15:

We praise God for this glorious month of June, the month of visitation of Fire and Power for divine settlement in all areas of our lives, in Jesus name.

I prophesy that as Moses and Mary received a special visitation from the Angel of The Lord to effect God's divine purpose for their lives, so will the same happen to you and your household, in Jesus name.(Exodus 3:1-2; Luke 1:26-28).

This visitation will end the sorrow, pain, misery, trouble and evil occurrence that have been harassing you, in Jesus name. This visitation begins your journey out of captivity and bondage into freedom and liberty.

This visitation will pronounce that your time of comfort is now, your time of Favour has come, and your time for manifestation of greatness is guaranteed, in Jesus name.

This visitation will be the fire of God that will refine, renew, revive, repair, restore and restructure your life and destiny and settle you forever, in Jesus name.

Fill your Spirit, meditate and declare: Luke 1:28,68; Genesis 21:1; Psalm 102:13; 106:4-5; 104:4; Deut 4:36; Malachi 3:2-3; Isaiah 66:15; Psalm 18:6-14.

BD No 16:

We thank the Great and Mighty God for this seventh month of Divine rest and perfection of everything committed to God since January to this July. As Solomon spoke, so I declare to you that God shall give us rest on every side and there will be neither adversary nor evil occurrence anymore, in Jesus name.

May your heart be glad and rejoice; May you forever rest in God's hope, faith and love till you see perfection in your life and destiny, and perfection of all your plans and expectations this year, in Jesus name.

I release the powerful force of the Spirit from the Altar of God to enter your life, home and community:

- To fight your battles, subdue and dominate darkness, in Jesus name.
- To turn around every challenge, enforcing satanic embargo, to stop and limit your steps to progress, in Jesus name.
- I speak prophetically that as the Spirit enters into you, move from ordinary to extra-ordinary;

- you will achieve victory in the second half of this year;
- everything the enemy meant for bad will turn around for your good;
- you will stand as a Woman of Purpose, Woman of Virtue, Woman of Substance, Woman of Treasure to take over territories and possess your possession, in Jesus name.

Understand, meditate and declare: 1 Kings 5:2-4; Isaiah 14:7; Amos 9:1; Ezekiel 2:2; 3:24; Psalm 18:32-33; Psalm 16:5-11; Exodus 33:14; Psalm 132:8; Proverbs 29:9; 24:15.

BD No 17:

May this new month of August be glorious, and as eight signifies new beginning, whatever has eluded you since January, you will begin to experience the fulfilment of God's promises, in Jesus name.

I decree that exceeding grace and favour will overwhelm you, no mistake or human error will stop the manifestation of your promises, in Jesus name.

As you journey through the last five months of this year, all your dreams will surely become a reality because the Altar of God is speaking for you, in Jesus name. All hindrances to your success will be removed; any stumbling block will become stepping stones to your greatness, in Jesus name. All what seems difficult, impossible or hard will become easy, smooth and possible, in Jesus name. The lines will fall for you in pleasant places, your feet will be like the feet of deer and you will ride upon your high places, in Jesus name.

Read and meditate on: Isaiah 43:19; Isaiah 40:1-5; Isaiah 41:18-20; Ezekiel 2:2; Psalm 18:32-33; Psalm 16:6; Psalm 71:21; Psalm 3:3; Psalm 66:12; 2 Samuel 22:1-3.

BD No 18:

We thank the great and mighty God for His faithfulness, goodness and mercies that endures forever.

We proclaim the manifestation of the blessing of wealth into every area of your life.

We connect you to the throne of grace and enforce blessings of multiplication, fruitfulness, increase, abundance of wealth in your spirit, soul and body, in Jesus name.

We decree the manifestation of wealth transfer is your portion in this time and season. No matter what your level is, may the supernatural force of God's Altar, begin to cause a turnaround for your upliftment and elevation to success, in Jesus name.

As Joseph moved from being a prisoner to a Prime Minister overnight, so will your change happen now, in

Jesus name. You will be lifted out of the dust and the dung hill to sit among princes and inherit the altar of glory, in Jesus name. (1 Samuel 2:8).

As Esther and Ruth experienced wealth transfer and changed history, so we declare the same supernatural transfer of the wealth stored up by sinners, for the just, is coming to you and your household, in Jesus name. (Proverbs 13:22; Isaiah 60.11).

All you need to do is believe, develop your understanding, and give yourself time to meditate on the WORD, live it, and speak it into existence. In Jesus Name.

BD No 19:

Glory be to God in the highest, for He rules and reigns forever in our lives.

We continue to proclaim the manifestation of the blessing of wealth in every area of our lives. In this last quarter, we secure our inheritance in The Blood Covenant. We enforce the blessings in Deuteronomy 32:13 that you will ride on the high places of the earth; eat the increase of the fields; suck honey out of the rock, and oil out of the flinty rock, in Jesus name.

As we stand together to declare the manifestation of wealth transfer in this time and season; I release the Spirit of Life in Christ Jesus and the supernatural force of God's Altar, to turnaround your situation for speedy manifestation of blessing, in Jesus name. If Ruth and Esther can move from being a hopeless widow and slave, to a wealthy woman and queen respectively, it is guaranteed your situation too will change and you will experience supernatural wealth transfer now, in Jesus name.

I speak that your gates shall be continually opened, they shall not be shut day nor night; that men will bring to you and your household the forces of the Gentiles and their kings in procession, in Jesus name.

Believe it! See it!! Speak it!! Receive it!!!

Read and Meditate on: Isaiah 60:11-18; Proverbs 13:22; Psalm 112:1-3; Deut 32:13.

BD No 20:

We give glory to the Lord Most High, who granted us the triple grace to begin this year well. May we remain in His presence and walk in righteousness, to enjoy all the goodness that God ordained for us, in Jesus name. Testimonies are pouring in of God's wonders, manifestations and fulfilments of blessings in our women's lives! I pray that God will satisfy everyone early with our hearts desires, and rejoice with gladness throughout this year, in Jesus name.

The Lord wants us to walk in His spiritual strength and power, to dominate in this year. As we are the light of this world, I pray our light will shine from within our spirit and soul, for the revelation, knowledge, deep understanding and wisdom; to direct, guide and order our steps to take the right actions that will birth our dreams, accomplish our assignment, and fulfil purpose, in Jesus name.

We need to ensure we give it all it takes to understand the importance of the Altar of God in our lives; how to keep the fire burning on the Altar; and how to keep invoking the power, and voice of the Blood of Jesus on the Altar continually forever.

Read, Meditate and Take action: 2 Corinth4:6; Ephesians1:17-20; 3:16-20; 5:8-14; Ps 43:3-4; Ps 118:27; Gen 22:9-18; Gen 35:3-7; Deut 27:5-7; Judges 6:22-26; 1 Chron 22:1; Rev 8:3; Amos 9:1.

BD No 21:

May the Lord bless you and keep you, make His face shine upon you and be gracious to you, lift up His countenance upon you and give you peace, In Jesus name.

We decree by the force of the power from God's Altar:

- Your destiny is fortified and uplifted to manifest the blessings of Asher;

- You will be the head, take charge and dominate wherever you go this year;

- You will be accepted in whatever you do to fulfil your purpose on earth, and you will eat the good of the land;

- We declare every virtue of the blessings of Asher will be your portion in your home, family, business, community churches and nations.

- We declare as you prophetically dip your feet in oil, you are protected and covered;

- Every enemy that will stand against you, God will destroy them. It doesn't matter how many forces or demonic animals that come against you, the hand of the Lord will destroy them; you are exempt from any imposed, intended, programmed or unexpected calamity, in Jesus name.

Everybody born of a woman will recognise and call you blessed; your destiny and everyone in your household will be ignited into unlimited blessings of fruitfulness, increase, abundance and multiplication, in Jesus name.

Read and Meditate on: Deut 33:24-29; Genesis 30:13; 49:20; Deut 32:13; Psalm 65:11; Psalm 36:7-8; Psalm 90:16-17; Psalm 37:22-23.

BD No 22: Mother's Day

Oh Lord our God how excellent is your name in all the earth. Thank you for March, the month of marching forward into fulfilment, as the Women and Mothers are celebrated this month.

May the Unprecedented Favour that transformed Esther from a slave girl to a Queen, locate you as we celebrate Mother's Day. Arise and move into new territories for promotion, progression and supernatural provision in all areas of your life, in Jesus name.

Woman, you are infused with power to forge ahead against all odds to take over, to take charge and to dominate; to confront and conquer any Haman plotting to terminate your assignment or destiny on earth, in Jesus name.

I decree and declare that:

- You are highly blessed; everyone born of a woman will call you blessed;

- The right hand of the Lord does valiantly, and will cover your head in the day of battle;

- You are anointed with fresh oil, and rivers of oil flow on your paths;

- You will break through barriers, blockages and demonic gates;

- You will possess the gates of your enemies;

- Your limitations, oppositions, frustrations, delays and denials are over;

- Your adversaries, principalities and powers are crushed;

- Your walls of Jericho have crumbled down, begin to jump forward;

- You will enter your promised land to possess treasures and hidden riches;

- You will encounter new doors of opportunities, and new realms;

- You will meet helpers, influencers and destiny lifters;

- You will be lifted to great heights of possibilities and power;

- The virtues of wisdom, strength, power, glory, honour and wealth will launch you into greatness;

- The wealth and riches of kings, princes, dignitaries and nobles will be transferred to you;

- As your glorious destiny is ignited, you will also spark other destinies into manifestation; In the mighty name of Jesus.

Shine as a true daughter of Zion, March forward in righteousness, holiness and the Word of Truth.

Read and Meditate on: Psalm 118:15; Luke 1:28; Proverbs 31:25-31; Psalm 144:12-15; Job 29:3-14)

BD No 23:

Through many unexplainable, unforeseen, unavoidable battles of life, we give thanks to God, for His mercies and compassions fail not. God's faithfulness, hope and love enable us to keep trusting him daily. We will not faint nor be weary, but renew our strength as we trust and wait patiently for His promises.

We will continue to stand strong in our faith; we will remain soldiers for Christ to aggressively fight Spiritual battles. We must remember to always resist the devil, and employ our spiritual weapons, to tread on serpents and scorpions and over all the power of the enemy.

For Life does not give you what you deserve, Life gives you what you demand! We are born again Christians, who pray and fast, but limited because of our faulty foundations, with many destinies trapped on the altars of our fathers' / mothers' houses. (Psalm 11:3; Lamentations 5:7-8).Life is not fair but God is faithful! He does not want us to linger on, endlessly in cycles of problems.

As we celebrate this Easter, I prophesy, that the anointing is released for you to experience a shift in all areas of your lives:

1. Power will change hands;
2. Altars and powers behind them will be broken;
3. Destinies will break free from yokes, burdens, oppressions, chains of injustice;
4. You will breakthrough and take back all you have lost;
5. Anointing of ease and sweat-less victory will overflow in your life, in The Name of Jesus.

This is the time for you to arise and take personal responsibility for your destiny and that of your loved ones!

Read and Meditate on: Isaiah 40:1-2, 29-31; Isaiah 25:7-8; Habakkuk 3:17-19; Job 13:15; Psalm 46:3-5; Luke 10:19; 1 John 3:8; Isaiah 52:1-2; Nehemiah 4:14.

BD No 24:

In this month of MAY:

May you find favour
May you find peace
May you find joy

May you find comfort

May you never fail

May you never weep

May you never lack

May you never be disgraced

May you find helpers

May you find humility

May you find honour

May you succeed

May you excel

May you be great, in the name of Jesus.

As you continue to stand to claim your deliverance and victory:

- I declare you are blessed in this month of **MAY** where:

M-miracle

A-await

Y-you

- For the set time to favour Zion has come. I declare this is your time; you will meet people in positions of authority who will go out of their way to help you, and work things out for your lifting;

- For it is time for your destiny to speak; you will be lifted, nothing can stop you, it will manifest now, in Jesus name;

- Receive the virtues, the strength, the wisdom, the glory, the honour, the riches, the power and the blessings.

- For God will do far more exceedingly than you ask or think, in Jesus name.

Read and Meditate on: Jeremiah 17:7-8; Psalm 102:13; Isaiah 58:10-11; 1Samuel 2:8; Psalm 18:32-33; Psalm 36:7-10; Psalm 90:16-17; Psalm 37:22-26. Rev 5:12.

BD No 25:

Praise The Lord the King of creations, for this beautiful month of June! God has granted the woman special favour, for visitation from the Angel of the Sixth month, to enforce our midst-season Blessings.

I release the force of light from God's Altar into your life and household, and decree and declare:

Your abundant blessing will overflow this month;

You are moving forward and nothing can stop you;

You shall not know sorrow, pain or calamity again;

Your Joy, Peace, Strength and Wisdom will overflow;

Your desires will manifest as you continue to delight in The Lord;

Your anointing will flow and move you to do exploits;

The good Lord will produce proofs and results that will terminate insults in your life, in Jesus name.

BD No 26:

We thank the Great and Mighty God, the Jehovah El Shaddai (God Almighty), Jehovah Rohi (God my Shepherd), Jehovah Nissi (God my Banner), for this seventh month of rest and perfection.

We thank God for a successful Women Conference, and pray that as you apply all the wisdom shared to Trim your Lamp, your Oil will never run dry; Your light will shine brighter and brighter and propel your destiny to greatness, in Jesus name.

As we enter the second half of this year, I prophesy a sweat-less life, a sweat-less victory, a sweat-less success for you and your household, in Jesus name. As Jabez prayed, and God changed his destiny from sorrow to blessing, so will God lift you out of every sorrow, pain, calamity, and enlarge your coast, in Jesus name.

As Ruth broke the curse of God on the Moabites, by following Naomi to partake of the covenant blessings, so I speak that any curse holding you as a lawful captive is broken and you are free, showers of blessing will overflow on you forever, in Jesus name.

BD No 27:

We thank God for this Month of August. The month of new beginnings and advancements into new, tangible and glorious things God is unveiling into our lives.

I decree and declare a tangible turnaround is going to happen in your life and destiny in these last five months. It cannot be denied, overlooked, avoided or restrained! It will locate you, overflow and overrun every area of your life and household, in Jesus name.

- The desires and expectations that you have not receive in the first seven months of the year, you will begin to take it by force now, in Jesus name;- Situations and circumstances that threatened your peace, progress, promotion and prosperity will turn around for your favour now;

- As The Lord rolled away the reproach of Egypt, so will everything that have reproached you and all your efforts, to achieve in the first seven months of this year, be rolled away now, in Jesus name.

I prophesy, in the remaining five months of this year you will be fulfilled with promotion and accelerated success - Spiritually, Professionally, Financially, Maritally, Physically and Health wise, in Jesus name.

- You will see your plans come to fruition; you will see your projects/programs and everything you lay your hands on will be successful;

- You will receive insight, revelation and ideas to move you into supernatural abundance, in Jesus name.

- You are going to the top, because you belong at the top!

- You were created to be in charge, therefore be lifted to the top and take charge of your destiny, in Jesus name.

BD No 28:

Glory be to God in the Highest, for He rules and reigns forever in our lives. As we continue to trust in the Lord, we shall be as mount Zion, which cannot be removed, but abides forever.

Today I pray, as we enter the last quarter of this year, your: Peace, Joy, Victory, Favour, Protection, Strength, Glory, Honour, Provision, Wisdom, Promotion, Power and Blessings will be forever, in Jesus name.

I declare according to Psalm 5:12: That you are surrounded with favour as a shield, so will you manifest speedily, supernatural blessings of wealth now, in Jesus name.

I speak that your gates shall be continually open, they shall not be shut, neither day nor night; that men, will bring to you and your household the forces of the Gentiles, and their kings in procession, in Jesus name.

Meditate and Declare: Isaiah 60:11-18; Proverbs 13:22; Psalm 112:1-3; Psalm 102:13; Isaiah 58:11; 1Samuel 2:8; Psalm 18:32-33

BD No 29:

We thank the Great and Mighty God for this month of November, and pray you will be a thousand times better, and blessed according to God's promise to Father Abraham on mount Zion, in Jesus name.

We decree and declare that the supernatural transfer of divine virtues, fortunes and treasures of the land flowing with milk and honey, is our portion;

We establish your life and household to be as mount Zion which cannot be removed but abide forever, in Jesus name. No matter what you are going through, I speak Peace, Joy, Strength, Wisdom, Protection, Provision, Promotion, Glory, Honour and Power will be the order of your life, from now on, in Jesus name.

I prophesy to you that as we approach the end of this year, you will see the goodness of the Lord every day, there shall be showers of blessings, your gates shall be continually opened and foreigners and strangers will build your walls. The sound of rejoicing and salvation will always be in your household; you will end this year strong, fulfilled and empowered, in Jesus name.

Meditate and Declare: Psalm 27:13-14; Eze 34:25-28; Isa 60:11-18; Ps 112:1-3; Ps 102:13; Isa 58:11; 1Sam 2:8; Ps18:32-33.

BD No 30:

Glory be to God in the Highest, for His abundant grace and faithfulness to enter this year. This is the year of manifestation of man's glory and the goodness of God, will crown the day. I assure you that God has great things in store for you this year that will silence your enemies forever, in Jesus name.

As you continue your journey throughout this year, and take your place in the kingdom:

- The Lord will hail you amongst your equals,

- You will be highly favoured,

- The Lord will be with you,

- You will be called blessed amongst women, in Jesus name.

The gate of this year is opened for you to walk through majestically, to accomplish your goals, achieve your divine purpose, take over territories, and occupy till Christ comes. I speak that so shall it be for you and me, in Jesus name. Anything that will stand in your way to obstruct, delay, limit or to stagnate you will be wasted, uprooted and crushed to pieces, by the Blood of Jesus.

I prophesy that God will guide you continually no matter the challenges, He will satisfy your soul in drought and strengthen your bones; and your destiny will be like a watered garden, and like a spring of water, whose waters will not fail, in Jesus name.

This year:

You will be satisfied;

You will be elevated;

You will be fulfilled;

You will dominate, in Jesus name.

Read and meditate on: Psalm 65:11; Luke 1:28,48; Isaiah 60:11; Isaiah 58:11; Psalm 112:1-3; Psalm 84:11; Malachi 4:2-3.

BD No 31:

We thank our Faithful God for this month of Perfection, Rest and Endless Favour.

According to Genesis 8:4, God will give you Rest on top of every mountain; Every situation of unrest in your life since the beginning of this year, I command it to cease and expire, in Jesus name.

Everywhere you go in this month, may every blessing that will bring you rest, locate you speedily, in Jesus name.

BD No 32:

May the Lord bless you and keep you, make His face shine upon you and be gracious to you, lift up His countenance upon you and give you peace, in Jesus name.

As we enter the 'ember' months, may you dominate in your promised land, may you recover all your ordained and expected blessings, in Jesus name; your open doors to greatness this year, will not pass you by because your Horn is exalted as you are anointed with fresh oil daily, in Jesus name.

As you subdue and overpower the giants in your promised land:

- Your glory will shine,

- Your horn will be exalted with honour,

- You will be crowned with Favour.

Everyone, everywhere and everything will minister favour upon favour unto you. As David became known and famous after killing Goliath, so I Prophesy your destiny will shine, you will be celebrated and honoured with supernatural wealth transfer, in Jesus name.

BD No 33:

We thank God for His faithfulness, we declare we shall be a thousand times better and blessed. God will make us ride on the high places of the earth, to eat the increase of the fields; to suck honey out of the rock, and oil out of the flinty rock, in Jesus name.

I decree and declare that you and your household are protected and secured, in the Blood of Jesus. No matter what the situation; tragedy and evil occurrences, programmed for the end of the year it will never locate your address.

Be encouraged, as it is written:

"It shall come to pass and your expectations shall not be cut off" - Proverbs 23:18;

"God is your refuge and strength, a very present help in trouble" - Psalm 46:1;

"Thou hast caused men to ride over our heads; we went through fire and through water: but thou brought us out into a wealthy place." - Psalm 66:12;

"Though my flesh and my heart faileth: but God is the strength of my heart, and my portion forever" - Psalm 73:

"God raises the poor from the dust and lifts the beggar from the ash heap, To set them among princes And make them inherit the throne of glory" - 1 Samuel 2:8;

"For God will light your candle: the Lord will enlighten your darkness.... It is God that arms you with strength, and makes your way perfect. He makes your feet like the feet of deer and sets you on your high places" - Psalm 18:28-29,32-33;In Jesus name.

BD No 34:

May the Lord bless you and keep you, make His face shine upon you and be gracious to you, lift up His countenance upon you and give you peace, in Jesus name, Amen.

As you continue into the last month of this year, I declare this season will bring you and your household: joy and gladness, glory and honour, favour and blessings, and you will end the year well, in Jesus name.

I decree and declare that The Voice of The Blood of Jesus will forever speak:

    - Grace upon Grace;
    - Peace that surpasses all understanding;

- Strength and Might;
- Endless mercies;
- Sure Protection and security;
- Exceeding great Power; to take you into
- Possibilities and greatness. In Jesus name.

Read and Meditate on: Genesis 32:13; Psalm 65:11; Habakkuk 3:17-19; Isaiah 49:2; Hosea 2:21-23; Malachi 4:2-3; Psalm 84:11.

BD No 35:

Glory! Glory! Alleluia, what a Mighty God we serve. God has been so good to us since we made the triumphant entry into this year.

God's wonder of manifold Blessings of rest on every side is flowing into all areas of our lives, in Jesus name.

May the strength and power to sail through the journey this year, be multiplied unto you, in Jesus name.

By the Anointing of God and by the voice of the Blood of Jesus, I decree and declare:

- The Lord will satisfy you early with His mercy, grace, joy, gladness, glory, honour, favour and riches;

- The Lord will establish you and secure your gates;

- The Lord will lift up your head, and where you have been silenced, your voice will become prominent;

- The God who shows up in the midst of troubles, will bring honey out of any rocky situation in your life;

- You will be great, and begin to do exploits to release the greatness in you;

-You will be celebrated beyond what you can imagine this year; In The Mighty Name of Jesus

BD No 36:

We thank the great and mighty God for His goodness and awesome power this month. You will experience rest on every side, and count your blessings daily, in Jesus name. God of all grace, has called you unto his eternal glory, no matter your situation, He will make you perfect, establish, strengthen, and settle you, in Jesus name. (1 Peter 5:10)

By the supreme power in the Blood of Jesus, you will see manifestation of the flow of blessings this year, in Jesus name.

I decree and declare:

- Your Joy will be full to overflowing;

- You will overcome your long-standing battle;

- The Lord mighty in battle, will continue to fight your battles and you will hold your peace;

- The God of all grace, will surely establish, strengthen and settle you to see the good of the land;

- Christ in you the hope of glory; God will increase you and comfort you on every side; In Jesus mighty name.

As God appeared as the fourth man in the fire, for Shedrach, Meshach and Abednego; so will God show up and bring you out of the fire, and long-standing battles will end forever, in Jesus name.

Arise, takeover, and dominate, for this is your time for favour and total restoration, in Jesus name.

BD No 37:

We give God all the glory, honour, power and praise for ushering us into the second half of the year beginning with July. Seven stands for perfection and rest, when God completed creation of the world and rested.

I decree and declare according to the unique date 7-7-17, It is a day of double perfection of God's glory and blessings on your life.

According to Micah 7:7 "Therefore I will look unto the LORD, I will wait for the God of my salvation: my God will hear me"

And Matthew 7:7 "Ask, and it shall be given you; seek, and ye shall find; knock, and it shall be opened unto you:"

- I decree that you will experience double perfection in spirit, soul and body, in Jesus name.

- As you look unto the LORD, and you wait for the God of your salvation, GOD will hear your prayers and perfect all that which concerns you, in Jesus name.

- As you ask, you shall receive, as you seek, you will find and as you knock, doors of greater opportunities shall be opened unto you perfectly, In Jesus name.

- I decree that your family, your job / profession / business, your health, your ministry, your finances, your marital life, and your children's education; will be made perfect by the Spirit of the most high God, in Jesus name.

According to Isaiah 7:7 "Thus saith the Lord God, It shall not stand, neither shall it come to pass."

- I decree an end to every evil released against you, that has determined to fight you from fulfilling your purpose shall no longer prosper, in Jesus name;

- Every confusion, controversy, contention, criticism, complaint, conniving and conspiracy against you, is cancelled, destroyed and the arrows return to sender, in Jesus name.

I stand in agreement with this writer that:

On the 7th DAY,
By the 7th HOUR,
At the 7th ROUND,
At the Blowing of the 7th TRUMPET,
By the 7th PRIEST.
The Wall of Jericho FELL DOWN FLAT.
Therefore, it is settled that everything harassing your progress; walls of Stagnation, Opposition, Sickness, Lack and Failure crumbles down before you now and forever, in Jesus name.

In the last six months of this year, you will turn them into stepping stones and rise to your greatness. You will be fulfilled and finish well, in Jesus name.

BD No 38:

All glory to our God for the grace and favour to have sailed through this year peacefully, and special thanks for the successful "Gathering of The Mighty" Conference. Bishop and Apostle's ministration filled us with power, anointing, wisdom and strategies to rise above satanic embargoes, and wax stronger to achieve all our plans and purposes, In Jesus name.

As we enter this festive season, I prophesy you have entered a new season of:

- joy and gladness,

- glory and honour,

- favour and blessings,

- possibilities and greatness,

- enlargement and Increase,

- empowerment and exploits, In Jesus name.

By the multitude of our sacrifices, power and fire from the Altar of God has released the voice to:

- fight all your battles;

- silence the ancestral, family, environmental altars and their strongmen/priests speaking satanic embargoes;

- bind and destroy witchcraft powers fighting you at all cost;

- revive, resurrect and restore every area of your life and destiny, in Jesus name.

Everyday till end of the year will be loaded with benefits, power, and blessings, in Jesus name.

You and your household are protected, your blessings are protected, your victory and breakthrough will manifest as you finish this well, strong, empowered and fulfilled, in Jesus name.

BD No 39:

Glory to the most high God for this month of endless mercy, grace and favour to manifest covenant blessings forever, in Jesus name. In this midst season, we decree that we will establish our dominion to fulfil all God's prophetic purposes, in the name of Jesus.

I decree and declare:

- You will experience the wonder of God;

- Your season of Joy and gladness, peace and love, glory and honour, favour and blessings, enlargement and Increase, total deliverance and emancipation will never cease;

-You are anointed to rise above situations and circumstances, all your personal battles have come to an end;

-You will overpower the giants, the 4 horns and witchcraft manipulations behind your personal battles;

-Your days of pain, problems, premature death, poverty and lack, struggle and hardship, sadness and sorrow, frustration and weaknesses, are over;

-God is your sun and shield, He gives you grace and glory all your days;

-He is the glory and the lifter of your head (Psalm 3:3b), He will deliver and restore you;

-Your time of favour has come, you are lifted to ride on the high places of the earth, elevated to inherit the altar of glory and be set among princes, in Jesus name.

BD No 40:

All Praises to God for His faithfulness through the Ember months. We Lift up the gate of every day in this season of harvest, and command our breakthrough into manifestation, in the name of Jesus.

We stand together in agreement and declare that we lift up the gates, for the King of Glory to come in and take His place in every area of our lives, in Jesus name.

I prophesy you will:

- Harvest bountifully in all your labour;

- Build and inhabit,

- Sow and reap,

- Be planted as trees of righteousness;

- Deliver all your proposed ideas and plans;

- Be fruitful and fulfilled;

- God will cause you to increase abundantly in Spirit, Soul and Body;

- Every arrow programmed to shed blood in the last months of this year will not locate you and your household;

- You will not suffer loss of lives, property, job, business, strength, power, and your spiritual place in God;

- God will crown you with goodness everyday as you walk the path of this year to the end; In The Mighty Name of Jesus.

BD No 41:

We thank the King of Kings, Lord of Lords, ancient of days for this glorious New Year, the year of fulfilment, fruitfulness and supernatural explosions for you and your household, in Jesus name.

I prophesy that:

- As you have started well, strong and empowered, you will be fulfilled in all your endeavours;

- God's supernatural strength, wisdom and courage will carry you through;

- You will be on top and shine throughout this year;

- Challenges are part of life but I decree, you will triumph over them all;

- God will turn you into a living surprise this year, because all that looked impossible last year will become easy this year;

- You will be blessed on time this year, no more delay, denial or disappointment, it is over;

- Your open doors, weddings, promotions, increase and enlargement, conceptions, good children, great opportunities, immigration settlement, etc will all be on time now, in Jesus name.

Isaiah 43:18-19 says "Do not remember the former things, Nor consider the things of old. Behold, I will do a new thing, Now it shall spring forth; Shall you not know it?

I will even make a road in the wilderness and rivers in the desert."

I prophesy in this New Year you will experience new ideas, new anointing, new employment, new businesses, new strength, new contacts, new connections, and new resources will flow, in Jesus name.

This year will be different; it will be your best year.

BD No 42:

We praise God for this month of May where Miracle Awaits You. May you continue to experience endless mercy, superlative grace and unprecedented favour, in Jesus name.

I prophesy speedy manifestation of all declarations released at the Easter conference in your life and household, in Jesus name.

According to Esther 2:17, I prophesy:

- The same grace on Esther will work for you, your spouse, children, health, workplace, business and ministry;

- Grace will be seen on you more than ever before, favour will always speak everywhere you go;

- As grace and favour crowned Esther, you will occupy your throne;

- Heaven will celebrate your enthronement into your next level;

- Your promotion to your new level is now. Every promotion you desire will be granted to you now;

- Queen Vashti was removed for Esther to take her place. Whoever is sitting, taking over, engaging or enjoying what belongs to you shall be unseated;

- Those holding what belongs to you will find it too hot to hold and release it to you;

- All the opportunities you have lost will be fully restored back now and forever, in Jesus name.

BD No 43:

We thank God for preserving us into the month of rest, victory and jubilation according to Leviticus 23:24. The siege is broken, and we will celebrate till the end of this year, in Jesus name.

We thank God for the "Women On Fire for Jesus" Conference. God's awesome presence, power and prophetic declarations, filled us with anointing of fire for us to make a difference in our lives, family, ministry, community and workplaces, in Jesus name.

I decree and declare your time of double portion of rest, victory and favour on every side has come.

According to Isaiah 54:2-3, I prophesy expansional Fire will saturate your life:

- Enjoy enlargement and increase in everything you do;

- God will enlarge your coast beyond your imagination;

- You will break-out, breakthrough and break-forth spiritually, financially, emotionally and maritally;

- This is your time to be promoted and lifted to your next level;

- Your mental capacity will grow to contain this increase;

- No more limitation, delay or failure at the edge of breakthrough;

- No more wastage, deprivation or destruction;

- Everything is turning around for your favour.

Enjoy your way till the end of this year; In Jesus Mighty name.

BD No 44:

Congratulations for your triumphant entry into the New Year and New Decade. Our good Lord ensured we made it gloriously into this year of supernatural expansion, enlargement and explosion in all areas of our life and household, in Jesus name.

I prophesy that this is your year and decade for enlargement and increase;

- You will expand on every side and your children shall inherit the land (Isaiah 54:2-3);

- Your year of God's double goodness, power, glory, honour and blessings is now;

- As you have started well, strong and empowered, all your goals and expectations will become manifestations;

- You will dwell in a good land, everywhere you go, you will see the goodness of the Lord in the land of the living;

- You will not know anymore lack, sorrow, pain or distress and you will be self-sufficient in your land (Deut 8:7–10);

- The strength, wisdom, favour and courage of God will sustain you;

- You will be on top and shine this year;

- According to Isaiah 43:18-19, I prophesy new things, new anointing, new sound health, new employment, new promotions, new businesses, new ideas, new contacts, new connections and new resources will flow to you throughout this year and decade, in Jesus name.

BD No 45:

All Glory to God for this month of marching forward into our expansion, enlargement and increase, in Jesus name.

I decree and declare on you and your household:

- Your year is crowned with goodness and all your pathways will flow with abundance (Psalm 65:11);

- You will enter a good land to eat in plenty and never lack (Deuteronomy 8:7-10);

- You will expand and increase in all areas of your life to gain your inheritance in the land (Isaiah 54:2-3);

- Your light will shine and the glory of the Lord will be seen no matter the darkness against you (Isaiah 60:1-2);

- The God of all grace that called you will work through any situation to perfect, strengthen and settle you (Psalm 65:11);

- The God of peace will give you rest and peace, for His Presence will always be with you (2 Thessalonians 3:16);

- The Lord will grant you the riches of His glory and strengthen you with might by His Spirit in your inner man; God will do far more exceedingly to make you productive, progressive and prosperous this year (Ephesians 3:16,20); In The Mighty Name of Jesus name.

BD No 46:

We praise the most high for the month of April, the season of Passover, when the power in the blood of Jesus was released for the deliverance of God's people. Surely, the pandemic of corona virus will Passover us, our families, communities and nations in this same season, in Jesus name.

As Daughters of Zion, we walk in the light and decree that:

- God will move this mountain of corona virus before us;

- God will turn this pandemic around by the power in the Blood;

- The expiry date for this pandemic is now and it will go this month;

- We decree no more deaths, destruction, distress and depression;

- Joy will come in the midst of pain and crying (Isa 61:3);

- We speak life to the nations across the earth (Rom 8:2);

- We speak healing to the nations, healing waters will flow (Rev 22:1-3);

- We speak restoration to families, communities and nations;

- We receive new joy and hope, we will enter the good land God has promised us (Deut 8:7-10);

- Our expectations for expansion and increase will not be cut off because of Covid19 (Isa 54:2-3);

- We decree good news of new beginnings during this pandemic, God will do a new thing (Isa 43:19);

- God will give us the Gold and Silver in this season (Haggai 2:8);

This Passover season, we declare as the children of Israel moved out of bondage to freedom in abundance, so shall it be for us too;

- No more shame, sorrow, sadness or slavery;

- We move out of slavery into Royalty (1 Samuel 2:8);

- We wear the garment, ring and crown of Royalty now (Psalm 45:13);

- Gates of divine elevation, doors of divine acceptance are opened into all areas of our lives (Isa 60:11);

- We are shining lights, an eternal excellence, the joy of many generations, in the name of Jesus. Amen.

BD No 47:

We give glory to God for abundant grace to witness this last month of the year. With the unprecedented period of COVID19 that lead to loss of lives, health, businesses, jobs, families, marriages, reputation, peace of mind, however, we thank God that as for you and I, we can say it's nothing missing, nothing broken, in Jesus name.

I decree and declare on you and your household:

D - Double portion;

E - Enlargement, Expansion and Increase;

C - Commitment and Consistency with God;

E - Energy for Exploits;

M - Multiplication;

B - Blessings in abundance;

E - Empowerment for lifting;

R - Revelations into new realms of power, possibilities and greatness.

I pray that whatever God has programmed for you this year that has not been deliver, will come to you before the end of this year, in Jesus name. May God restore and compensate you and I for whatever we have lost during the pandemic period, in Jesus name.

BD No 48:

All glory to God for guiding us into the season of Passover and Easter celebration, of the resurrection of our Lord Jesus Christ. May you encounter continuous victories, as the resurrection power quickens your financial, health, family, marital and children's life unto glory and honour, in Jesus name.

I prophesy that the power of the speaking and sprinkling Blood of Jesus, will be activated, in warfare for your complete victory and breakthrough, in the name of Jesus.

I decree and declare that:

- Satanic ordinances are silenced forever;

- Agent of death through COVID19, terrorism, ritual killings, knife and gun crime and violence, are silenced and banished forever;

- Restoration of wasted years;

- Cancellation of debts;

- The rest of your years, will not be in struggle but prosperity;

- Your voice will override the voice of your enemies;

- The rod of the wicked is broken, and will not rest on your lot again;

- God will mitigate your adverse experiences, and restore you abundantly;

- You will be lifted from obscurity and your destiny will shine;

Enjoy Open Heavens of Blessings! In The Mighty Name of Jesus.

BD No 49:

We thank God for this season, and decree that we will manifest rest on every side, amidst the wickedness looming across the nations.

God has promised rest for His people, and so shall it be in our lives, in Jesus name.

Glory be to God for a successful Women's Conference, that endowed us with power to exercise our authority as a Lioness.

I prophesy according to Hebrews 4:9-11, 1 Kings 5:4, and Isaiah 30:15 that:

- You will have complete rest that can never be denied;

- You will live in peace and dwell in God's safety;

- You and your household will always be saved, as you return into His rest;

- Your quietness and confidence in His rest shall be your strength;

- In His rest, you will be comforted and increase your greatness;

- The Lioness ability to protect will be your strength, as a virtuous woman;

- Your roar as a Lion ends the era of adversary, and evil occurrence forever;

- As a Lion take over its territories, your family, marital life, children, health, finances, investments, spiritual life, will no longer suffer loss;

- You will forever be in charge and have dominion, as you exhibit your love, obedience, fear and trust for God; In The Mighty Name of Jesus.

BD No 50:

We thank our faithful God, for this glorious year. We honour and worship the Alpha and Omega (beginning and the end), the Jehovah Elshaddai (God almighty), the Rock of Ages, the Lion of the Tribe of Judah, the God who holds our everyday. Oh God, keep your heavens open over us throughout this year, in Jesus name.

May we receive grace to remain faithful to God, who has the perfect knowledge of who we are, and has the number of our days already recorded in His Book (Psalm 139:16);

May all your plans, goals, expectations for this year come to fruition;

May this New Year bring new opportunities, new strength, new power, new knowledge, new understanding, new wisdom, and new vision helpers;

May God end every negative experience of past years. There will be no more cry, no more pain, no more losses, no more agony, no more tragedy, no more trauma in your life;

May God disconnect you from anyone or association going backward, and connect you to pacesetters and brilliant minds;

May God turn around the tables before your enemies for your favour, after the order of Esther and Mordecai (Esther 8:12-13);

May your gates be continually open, day and night, that men may bring to you the wealth of the Gentiles and their kings in procession;

May your life be sweet and full of taste, you will suck honey from every avenues open to you;

May rivers of oil pour out on every step you take, and every path be full of the fatness for you and your household; In The Mighty Name Of Jesus.

BD No 51:

We thank our Magnificent God for this special month of February, with the prophetic No 2, for double blessings of Open Heavens. The calendar shows three dates with five 2s, meaning double grace is our portion now and forever, in Jesus name.

Genesis 7:11; 8:14-17 established our open heavens and the earth yielding abundance, fruitfulness and multiplication in our lives, in the name of Jesus.

I prophesy according to Hosea 2:21-22, that your Open Heavens will manifest double Grace for you and your household to overflow:

- Grace for continuous blessings of peace, joy, salvation, healing, deliverance, restoration and breakthrough;

- Grace for prosperity in your spirit, soul and body;

- Grace for constant provision, protection, progress and preservation;

- Grace for consistent spiritual strength and power;

- Grace for spiritual advancement and growth;

- Grace for supernatural turnaround to goodness and favour;

- Grace for everyday good news, good tidings and good radiance;

- Grace for the more than enough blessings, that located Esther, Ruth, Joseph and David will overwhelm you; In Jesus Mighty Name.

BD No 52:

Oh Faithful God, thank you for standing sure, safe, secure, strong and solid with us into this month of June.

The bible says in:

Haggai 1:1 "In the first day of the sixth month the word of the Lord came to Zerubbabel"

Luke 1:26-28: In the sixth month the Angel Gabriel was sent to.... the virgin Mary;

Ezekiel 8:1: And it came to pass, in the sixth year, in the sixth month in the fifth day...the hand of the Lord God fell upon Ezekiel.

I prophesy, in the name of Jesus, this sixth month, divine visitation and supernatural encounters will overwhelm you:

- to hail, honour, bless and exalt you;

- to bring you good news and your heart felt desires;

- to establish you in righteousness, goodness and truth;

- to secure your portion of the profit of the earth;

- to give you a voice to override the voice of your enemies;

- to bring the hand of Lord upon your adversaries;

- to reverse back to sender every evil projection;

- to restore back all that has been stolen;

- to miraculously turnaround everything for your favour;

- to strengthen and perfect your way to stand as the Mary, Esther, Deborah, Ruth, of your generation in Jesus mighty name.

BD No 53:

All glory, honour, power and praise to God for this month of August. The month of new beginning, and manifestation of the Supernatural, from the successful Prophetic Conference. We decree there shall be a performance of all the prophetic release of blessings, in all areas of our life for Salvation, Healing, Deliverance, Victory, Protection, Peace, Joy and Gladness, Favour and Restoration, in Jesus name.

I prophesy according to Deuteronomy 8:7-10, that:

Your new beginning is taking you to a new land of opportunities, surplus provision and abundant supply for you and your household, in the name of Jesus:

A new land where:

- all your prophetic blessings will become manifestations;

- you will count your blessings in the last 5 months of this year;

- you will enjoy goodness, greatness and gladness;

- you will have rest on every side from all wars, tragedies and disasters around;

- you will see no more drought and famine but fruitfulness;

- every wilderness situation is turned around to garden of the Lord;

- you will see no more lack and insufficiency but eat in plenty;

- your expectations will not be cut off but shall come to fruition;

- you will grow spiritually, emotionally, financially, physically and relationally;

- you will be fulfilled in your divine assignment, purpose and destiny; In the mighty name of Jesus.

BD No 54:

Glory be to the King of kings, the Governor over the Nations (Psalm 22:28) We thank God for September to Remember of the New era of a New King, New Prime Minister and New season. We declare a supernatural shift and open heavens over the destiny of the UK, to impact our lives for peace and prosperity, power and purpose, in the name of Jesus.

We stand and prophesy:

Proverbs 8:15-16 "By me kings reign, And princes decree justice. By me princes rule, And nobles, even all the judges of the earth." That the 70th year, reign of the Late Queen for good service, peace and provision in the land, will be multiplied in this New Era of governance and ruler-ship in Jesus name;

1 Chronicles 12:32 "And of the children of Issachar, which were men that had understanding of the times, to know what Israel ought to do" That there will be increased understanding to establish Gods agenda for revival, redemption, restoration and righteousness in the nation in Jesus name;

Proverbs 14:34 "Righteousness exalteth a nation: but sin is a reproach to any people." That the nation will be lifted and exalted, the new kingship and leadership will operate in righteous, justice and compassion, in Jesus name;

Proverbs 21:1 "The king's heart is in the hand of the Lord, as the rivers of water: he turneth it whithersoever he will." That the King of Kings will be in control of the New King, to walk in the fear, wisdom of God, and influence of the Holy Spirit, in Jesus name;

Jeremiah 29:7 "And seek the peace of the city whither I have caused you to be carried away captives, and pray unto the Lord for it: for in the peace there of shall ye have peace." That we will experience peace and prosperity across the nation in homes and families, children and youths, community and development, business and economics, in Jesus name;

Psalm 33:5 "He loveth righteousness and judgment: the earth is full of the goodness of the Lord." That as you seek righteousness and justice in this new era, you will see the goodness of the Lord, and enter your new levels, of open doors, opportunities, contracts, connections, relationships, victories and triumphs. In the mighty name of Jesus.

BD No 55:

The Grace of God has brought us through this year, crowned us with goodness and mercy, and success in our endeavours, and all our conferences, in Jesus name.

As we celebrate this festive season,

- The Goodness and faithfulness of God will overwhelm you;

- Faith that makes things possible will not fail you;

- Mercy that makes all sins forgiven will speak for you;

- Hope that makes all things work will answer for you;

- Favour that makes things turnaround will colour your life;

- Grace that makes all things abound will be sufficient for you;

- Love that makes all things beautiful, will be your banner, in Jesus Name.

I decree and declare that you and your household will end this year well, strong, fulfilled and empowered to start 2023, in the name of Jesus:

-You will be full of good health, spiritual health, emotional health, financial health;

-You will grow with a sound mind and intellectual strength;

-You will walk in spiritual might, insight and revelation power;

- You will wax strong and do exploits for the Kingdom of God;

No matter what is happening with you or around the world:

- You will not see tragedy, calamity nor destruction anymore;

- You will see the Joy and Salvation of the Lord always;

- You will not be frustrated, faint, fear, fail or fall;

- You will be protected, preserved and surrounded with songs of deliverance;

- You will arise in Power and Strength of God daily to fulfil your purpose, in the mighty name of Jesus.

BD No 56:

All glory to God for bringing us into the midst season again, where His divine visitation will revive our spiritual, emotional, mental, health, marital and financial strength; by His Mercy and Grace in Jesus name.

Ezra 7:9 and Genesis 21:1 says;

> *"For upon the first day of the first month began he to go up from Babylon, and on the first day of the fifth month came he to Jerusalem, according to the good hand of his God upon him."*

"And the LORD visited Sarah as he had said, and the LORD did unto Sarah as he had spoken."

I prophesy:

- The hand of God shall be upon your life to lift you out of obscurity to prosperity;

- Every Babylonian situation is turned around in your life;

- All the goodness and bounties due to you since January is restored back to you;

- God's visitation will bring you into Jerusalem:

your place of glory,

your season of abundance,

your position of greatness;

- As God had spoken, enjoy new life of peace, joy, progress and open doors;

- The grace and favour released by the King to "restore all that was hers" (Shunammite woman Estate), shall be multiplied to you and your household too in Jesus name;

- Every power behind any evil assignment to swallow your inheritance, be scattered by the blood, fire and Gods vengeance in the mighty name of Jesus. Amen.

BD No 57:

We thank our faithful God, for making us triumph gloriously into the year of Perfection, Multiplication and Fruitfulness. Oh faithful God by your mercy and grace, keep your heavens open over us throughout this year, in the name of Jesus.

Oh God of creation, who holds the air we breathe, who has the perfect knowledge of man, who has the number of our days already recorded in His Book, Psalm 139:16, help us to remain faithful and consecrated to you this year.

Oh gracious and sweet Lord, make this year extremely glorious for us. Make our life sweet and full of taste, help us to suck honey out of the rocks always.

Oh God the master builder make all our plans, goals, expectations and desires come to reality this year.

Oh God that does new things, bring new things, new strength, new power, new knowledge, new understanding, new wisdom, new opportunities and new vision helpers into our lives.

Oh God the Mighty Man in battle,

- Bring to an end every negative experience of previous years. There will be no more crying, pain, losses, agony, tragedy, and trauma this yea;

- Disconnect us from anyone or association of backwardness, and connect us to brilliant minds moving forward.

- Turn around the tables before our enemies for our favour, after the order of Esther and Mordecai;

Oh God that makes a way where there is no way, let our gates be opened continually, both day and night.

Let rivers of oil pour out on every step we take and fill our path with fatness of the land this year, in The Mighty Name of Jesus.

BD No 58:

All Praises to our Awesome God for His mercies towards us are great, for guiding us through the 1st quarter of this year, Father we thank you;

For your loving kindness and faithfulness of peace, provision, protection and prosperity we thank you;

For a successful Easter conference, with signs and wonders following, we thank you;

For Bishop Chigbundu's 70 years of a fulfilled life on this earth, we thank you;

For the manifestation of your power, promises and prophecies, we thank you;

For keeping us through the fire and raging storms of life, we thank you;

For showing yourself strong amidst the battles against Israel and Christianity, we thank you;

For strengthening us by your Spirit in our inner man, to keep up the journey until we receive our Inheritance, we thank you;

For the great things you will do for thy Kingdom come and your Will be done, in our lives, families, communities and nations, Father we thank you.

I declare, you are a Powerful Woman on the Altar! Do not cast away your confidence! no more fear, sadness, shame or frustration! Keep your hope alive by truly loving, obeying, fearing and trusting in God. Psalm 37:3-5

God has your back. He will never leave you nor forsake you (Hebrews 13:5), In Jesus Mighty Name.

BD No 59:

Magnificent and Awesome God, we thank you for May, the fifth month that begins the midst season of this year. Five stands for Grace and we declare the garment of Grace will cover us and our households, in this time and season, in the name of Jesus.

According to Ezra 7:9:

> *"For upon the first day of the first month began he to go up from Babylon, and on the first day of the fifth month came he to Jerusalem, according to the good hand of his God upon him."*

I prophesy that as we travail together on God's Altar in this season:

- The hand of God shall be upon your life, for God releasing His power to manifest your glorious destiny;

- The hand of God shall take you up out of every Babylon situation, and bring you to your promised land;

- The powers that kept you in Babylon will be destroyed and devoured at once;

- The Altar of God will roar against everything representing Babylon and you will prevail against them and be free;

- The hand of God will turn around the situation, and conditions, troubling you and your household, into your favour;

- Your goodness and harvest that Babylon has swallowed, will be restored back now and forever;

- The hand of God and Power of His Altar is progressing you into your Jerusalem, a place of fruitfulness and abundance forever;

- No more sorrow, sadness and shame, will enter you, your new life is full of peace, joy, laughter, progress, prosperity and testimonies;

- The hand of God will multiply the same Favour enjoyed by Esther, Ruth, Hannah, Deborah, Abigail, Mary and Elizabeth into your life and household; In The Mighty Name of Jesus.

BD No 60:

As we step into a new month, I prophesy:

1) MANIFESTATION OF ANGELIC ENCOUNTERS

According to Luke 1:26, 28

> *"And in the 6th month the angel Gabriel was sent from God unto a city of Galilee, named Nazareth And the angel came in unto her, and said, Hail, thou that art highly favoured, the Lord is with thee: blessed art thou among women."*

You will be highly favoured and blessed to standout among your tribe, in Jesus name.

2) REVELATION & VISITATION

According to Ezek 8:1-3:

> *"And it came to pass in the sixth yr, in the sixth month, in the 5th day of the month, as I sat in mine house, & the elders of Judah sat before me, that the hand of the Lord God fell there upon me. Then I beheld, and lo a likeness as the appearance of fire: from the appearance of his loins even downward, fire; and from his loins even upward, as the appearance of brightness, as the colour of amber. And He put forth the form of an hand, & took me by the lock of mine head; & the spirit lifted me up between the earth & the heaven & brought me in the visions of God to Jerusalem."*

The visitation of God and the Fire of His presence will rest on you, and your household, in Jesus name.

3) ACCOMPLISH HIS GREAT DEEDS

Haggai 1:1,14

> *"In the second year of King Darius, in the sixth month, on the first day of the month, the word of the Lord came by Haggai the prophet to Zerubbabel the son of Shealtiel, governor of Judah, and to Joshua the son of Jehozadak, the high priest, saying, So the Lord stirred up the spirit of Zerubbabel the son of Shealtiel,*

*governor of Judah, and the spirit of Joshua the
son of Jehozadak, the high priest, and the spirit
of all the remnant of the people; and they came
and worked on the house of the Lord of hosts,
their God,"*

You will accomplish great deeds for the glory of God, in
Jesus name.

Chapter Two

MOTHERS' DECLARATIONS

<u>DAILY DECLARATIONS</u>

As a Mother, Oh Lord I arise daily to declare over my entire household Psalm 118:15, 24

"The voice of rejoicing and salvation is in the tabernacles of the righteous: the right hand of the Lord doeth valiantly. This is the day which the Lord hath made; we will rejoice and be glad in it."

I command the day to declare, this is the day the Lord as made, we will rejoice and be glad throughout the day.

We will experience the goodness of the Lord everyday; I declare as for me and my house we will serve the Lord, the right hand of the Lord will do valiantly for us.

God's presence fills our home and His mighty power brings salvation, healing, deliverance, victory and overflowing Joy into manifestation in this home, in Jesus name.

I declare according to 1 John 4:4 and Jeremiah 29:11

"You are of God, little children, and have overcome them, because He who is in you is greater than he who is in the world."

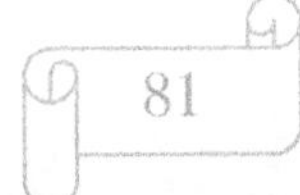

- I arise in power to declare God's plan, purpose and promise over our lives will be established;

- I arise in power to speak possibilities, opportunities, and open doors into every area of our lives;

- I arise in power to declare the spirit of the Lord is upon us, and God is in full control over our lives;

- I arise as the intercessor of my home, that I will remain strong in the Lord and in the power of His might, to ensure God's Kingdom come and Will is done in this home, in Jesus name.

I declare according to Hebrews 12:24 and Revelation 1:5

"to Jesus the Mediator of the new covenant, and to the blood of sprinkling that speaks better things than that of Abel."

"from Jesus Christ, the faithful witness, the firstborn from the dead, and the ruler over the kings of the earth. To Him who loved us and washed us from our sins in His own blood,"

- We cover our Spirit, soul and body with the Blood of Jesus and put on the whole armour of God;

- Oh Lord cleanse us, purify us, sanctify us holy and acceptable unto you in the name of Jesus.

- We cover our entire household, houses and environment up to 500 metres radius with the blood of Jesus; we take authority over the atmosphere and command it is cleansed from every infiltration of darkness, in Jesus name.

I declare according to Ephesians 2:13 and Revelations 12:11

> *"But now in Christ Jesus you who once were far off have been brought near by the blood of Christ."*

> *"And they overcame him by the blood of the Lamb and by the word of their testimony, and they did not love their lives to the death."*

- Everywhere we go, we move in the pool of the Blood of Jesus and exercise our authority to command that Peace and Blessings of the Lord is our portion, only the good, the great, and the glorious things will come into our lives in Jesus name.

- We stand on the ground of the Blood of Jesus, to declare victory over sin, Satan, it's agents and the world in Jesus name.

- We sprinkle the Blood of Jesus into the spirit realm to stop every satanic and demonic activities operating against us, we pull down, throw down, uproot and destroy them according to Jeremiah 1:10

> "See, I have this day set thee over the nations and over the kingdoms, to root out, and to pull down, and to destroy, and to throw down, to build, and to plant." In Jesus Name.

- We stand on the ground of the Blood of Jesus, to declare victory over any evil programming, evil plans, evil pronouncement, evil predictions, evil prophecies; through dreams or in the physical in Jesus name.

- We enforce that we enter a new day of possibilities, opportunities, open doors, that all spiritual blessings in heavenly place will magnetise to us, in the name of Jesus.

I superimpose the prophetic purposes of God and enforce my dominion that my voice will override the voice of my enemies; according to Psalm 8:2 & 6

> *"Out of the mouth of babes and nursing infants You have ordained strength, Because of Your enemies, That You may silence the enemy and the avenger."*

> *"You have made him to have dominion over the works of Your hands; You have put all things under his feet,"*

I speak a turnaround to all circumstances and situations, that confront me today;

- I am not a victim, I am a victor;

- I am not weak, I am strong;

- I am not sick, I am healed;

- I am not poor, I am rich;

- I am not a destitute; I am destined to win;

- I am not a worrier; I stand on the word;

- I am not fearful; I am full of faith;

- I am not a burden; I am a blessing; In Jesus Name.

I have the spirit of power, love and a sound mind. I will take the right decisions to shape my destiny.

No more errors, no more mistakes, no more failure, because the Spirit of the Lord is upon me, the spirit of wisdom and understanding, the spirit of counsel and might, the spirit of knowledge and the fear of the Lord, fills our lives (Isaiah 11:2).

I walk with a victorious mindset, and declare my thoughts, my words; my actions will be in divine alignment with the will of God. I will take the right decisions that will make me powerful, and bring progress into all areas of my life, in Jesus name.

Grace, Favour and Mercy of the Lord Jesus Christ, will be multiplied unto me and my household every day, hour, minute, second of our lives, In the mighty name of Jesus.

COMMANDED BLESSINGS

According to Deuteronomy 28:8

"The LORD will command the blessing on you in your storehouses and in all to which you set your hand, and He will bless you in the land which the LORD your God is giving you."

Psalm 42:8 "The LORD will command His loving kindness in the daytime, and in the night His song shall be with me— A prayer to the God of my life."

Genesis 49:25-26 "Even by the God of thy father, who shall help thee; And by the Almighty, who shall bless thee With blessings of heaven above, Blessings of the deep that lieth under, Blessings of the breasts, and of the womb. The blessings of thy father have prevailed above the blessings of my progenitors, unto the utmost bound of the everlasting hills. They shall be on the head of Joseph, and on the crown of the head of him that was separate from his brethren."

Genesis 1:27-28 "So God created man in His own image; in the image of God He created him; male and female He created them. Then God blessed them, and God said to them, "Be fruitful and multiply; fill the earth and subdue

I decree and declare that:

- I am blessed

- My children and family are blessed

- The labour of my hands are blessed

- My employment, employer and fellow employees are blessed

- I am blessed with good health

- I am blessed with a good marriage

- I am blessed with a great happy home

- I am blessed with a good job, profession, career, and business

- I am blessed with a good car

- I am blessed going out, and blessed coming in

- Everywhere I go I am blessed

- Everything I touch, is blessed

- Everyone that comes in contact with me is blessed

- My Pastor is blessed

- My neighbours are blessed

- My mentor and coach are blessed

- My doctor, lawyer, teacher, fitness trainer, mechanic, driver, nurse, carers, cleaners, gardener, are all blessed

- My Church is blessed

- All my fellow brethren are blessed. In The Name of Jesus.

POSITIVE SELF TALK

- I am the best

- I can do it

- God is always with me

- I am a Winner

- Today is my day

- I am productive

- Everything I lay my hands to do will prosper

- I am an amazing worker

- People love, value and respect my work and creations

- I am paid very well for doing what I love to do

- I will have peace and rest

- I am destined for greatness

- I have the mind of a billionaire

- I will operate without stress; life will be easy for me

- I am not a victim, I am a victor;

- My life will be sweet;

- I am anointed to fulfil destiny;

- I value money, and I will attract money that will meet all my needs;

- Money is good for me; I will accomplish my goals and it will bring me wealth;

- I am kind, I am generous, I can use money to contribute more good to the world.

<u>Positive Self Talk to get rid of negativities (unforgiveness, abuse, anxiety)</u>

- I forgive you

- I am sorry

- Thank you

- I love you

- You are blessed

Note:
Make sure you always meditate on the word of God;
Keep speaking positive things consistently;
Trust in God for a change always; In Jesus name.

PRAYERS / DECLARATIONS FOR CHILDREN and YOUNG PEOPLE

1) Oh Lord we thank you for the lives of our children and youths in Jesus name. We bring all our concerns over them before you and thank you for you are in perfect control of their lives in Jesus name.

1b) Oh Lord Bless our children in their education, health, employment, career, profession, potentials & talents in Jesus name.

2) We cover our children and youths always with the Blood of Jesus and we put the whole armour of God upon them in Jesus name.

> Ephesians 6:10-12 "Finally, my brethren, be strong in the Lord, and in the power of his might. Put on the whole armour of God, that ye may be able to stand against the wiles of the devil. For we wrestle not against flesh and blood, but against principalities, against powers, against the rulers of the darkness of this world, against spiritual wickedness in high places."

2b) By the Power in the Blood of Jesus, We separate our children from the wickedness in the world around them, in Jesus name.

2c) We set our children free from any power assigned to afflict their souls by divination and witchcraft in Jesus name.

By the Blood I separate you, By the Blood I pull you out of darkness, in the name of Jesus.

3) We pray for the redemption of their soul, that they will receive Christ early in life.

We make a demand Oh Lord, by the Blood for total redemption of our children's soul. Oh Lord separate them from darkness & count them worthy to enter into the kingdom of your dear Son, in Jesus name.

4) We pray the Holy Spirit will be poured on them and their lives will be a place of abode for the Holy Spirit, in Jesus name.

5) Oh God arise in your power and arrest the hearts of children and youths facing challenges that they will totally submit to God and turn from Satan, in Jesus name.

5b) We pray they will have a heart that will obey God, fear God and serve God with all their soul. That they will be willing to be sold out for Jesus.

Father pour your clean water upon them, give them a new heart Oh Lord, in Jesus name.

6) We pray that they will develop a strong faith and hold on to their Christian beliefs when they are with friends.

6b) Oh God, give them strength to resist temptation and grant them boldness to stand in righteousness.

Strength to say no and never go back to their old ways, in the name of Jesus.

7) We break the power of peer pressure, by the power in the blood of Jesus. We pray that they will desire the right kind of friends and be protected from wrong friends, in Jesus name.

8) We break the power of the world, lust, pervasion, wrong desires and evil counsel upon our children and youths always, and pray that they will have hatred for sinful things in Jesus name.

9) We break the negative power flowing through the education system, media, music, television, internet & social media always on our children and youths, in Jesus name.

10) Oh Lord protect them from the evil one, always direct their steps, guide and prevent them from falling into the enemy's traps, in Jesus name.

Protect them Oh lord, from Barons, strongmen initiating them into evil;

They will not fall into the traps, snares, cage set for them;

- Deaths wrapped as presents, be exposed and destroy;
- Poison presented as perfume, be exposed and destroyed;
- Enemies appearing as friends, be exposed and destroyed;
- Girlfriends appearing as Delilah, Jezebel, be exposed and destroyed;

- Boyfriends appearing as Err, Omnana, Amnon, be exposed and destroyed;

We pull them out from the cage of the enemy, in the name of Jesus. We declare:

Jeremiah 31:16b&17 "they shall come again from the land of the enemy. And there is hope in thine end, saith the Lord, that thy children shall come again to their own border."

Zechariah 10:8 "I will whistle for them and gather them, For I will redeem them; And they shall increase as they once increased."

John 10:5, 27 "Yet they will by no means follow a stranger, but will flee from him, for they do not know the voice of strangers." "My sheep hear My voice, and I know them, and they follow Me."

Exodus 23:2 "You shall not follow a crowd to do evil; nor shall you testify in a dispute so as to turn aside after many to pervert justice."

We break our children and youths free from the cage of the enemy, in Jesus name.

11) Oh God reveal what is going on in our children and youths lives always. We command all hidden secrets of the enemy to be exposed by the light of God. And that they will be caught when guilty of doing wrong, in Jesus name.

12) Oh God arise in your power and arrest the hearts of our children, they will not be lost in the world, in Jesus name.

> *Psalms 80:17-19 "Let thy hand be upon the man of thy right hand, upon the son of man whom thou madest strong for thyself. So will not we go back from thee: quicken us, and we will call upon thy name. Turn us again, O Lord God of hosts, cause thy face to shine; and we shall be saved."*

13) We take authority and break them free from generational curses and ancestral evil inheritance. We renounce, revoke, destroy evil covenants and disconnect them from every evil flow from their parent's background forever, in Jesus name.

14) We take authority and break the strength of the Ancestral strongman that has programmed rebellion, failure, poverty, non-achievement and destruction unto their destinies, in Jesus name.

> *Isaiah 49:24-26 "Shall the prey be taken from the mighty, Or the captives of the righteous be delivered? But thus says the Lord: "Even the captives of the mighty shall be taken away, And the prey of the terrible be delivered; For I will contend with him who contends with you,*

15) We command every demon and wicked spirits operating behind curses, covenants, spells, bewitchment and all witchcraft activities to be bound and cast out by the fire of God in Jesus name.

15b) Powers assigned to turn our children into arrows in our hearts instead in our hands, receive fire, we pull you down, in Jesus name.

Powers assigned to waste children's destinies; turn them into vagabonds or wanderers on the earth; turn them into servants for their mates; trade their souls in satanic markets; Be destroyed and receive judgement of fire, in Jesus name.

16) We cancel any negative words spoken, evil prophecies and vows released over our children and youths, by the power in the blood of Jesus, in Jesus name.

All Evil tares, thorns & thistles sown by words we uproot and destroy it;

We forbid witchcraft from using these words against them. We bind the demon holding the words to operate in the future of our children, in Jesus name.

17) We replace every curse, negative words, evil programming, etc with God's blessings always on our children and youths, in Jesus name.

Psalm 112:1-3 "Praise ye the Lord. Blessed is the man that feareth the Lord, that delighteth greatly in his commandments. His seed shall be mighty upon earth: the generation of the upright shall be blessed. Wealth and riches shall be in his house: and his righteousness endureth for ever."

Isaiah 60:15-16 "Whereas you have been forsaken and hated, So that no one went through you, I will make you an eternal excellence, A joy of many generations. You shall drink the milk of the Gentiles, And milk the breast of kings; You shall know that I, the LORD, am your Saviour And your Redeemer, the Mighty One of Jacob.

Isaiah 60:18 "Violence shall no more be heard in thy land, wasting nor destruction within thy borders; but thou shalt call thy walls Salvation, and thy gates Praise."

Isaiah 58:11 "The LORD will guide you continually, And satisfy your soul in drought, And strengthen your bones; You shall be like a watered garden, And like a spring of water, whose waters do not fail."

18) We pronounce that they will be **ARROWS IN OUR HANDS**, sharp Arrows of blessing, favour, honour, power and praise to their parents, families and their generation, in Jesus name.

Psalm 127:4-5 "Like arrows in the hand of a warrior, So are the children of one's youth. Happy is the man who has his quiver full of them; They shall not be ashamed, But shall speak with their enemies in the gate."

Isaiah 8:18 "Here am I and the children whom the LORD has given me! We are for signs and wonders in Israel From the LORD of hosts, Who dwells in Mount Zion."

Psalm 45:2 "You are fairer than the sons of men; Grace is poured upon Your lips; Therefore God has blessed You forever."

Psalm 147:13 "For He has strengthened the bars of your gates: He has blessed your children within you."

19) We confess that they will be filled with Wisdom, Knowledge and Understanding to excel in their generation, in Jesus name.

Isaiah 11:2 "The Spirit of the LORD shall rest upon Him, The Spirit of wisdom and understanding, The Spirit of counsel and might, The Spirit of knowledge and of the fear of the LORD."

Job 32:8 "But there is a spirit in man, And the breath of the Almighty gives him understanding."

Ephesians 1:18 "the eyes of your understanding[a] being enlightened; that you may know what is the hope of His calling, what are the riches of the glory of His inheritance in the saints,"

Luke 2:52 "And Jesus increased in wisdom and stature, and in favour with God and men."

20) We declare that everywhere our children and youths go, they will be recognised as those whom the lord has blessed. They will have responsible attitudes and people will go out of their way to help and favour them.

Isaiah 61: 9 "Their descendants shall be known among the Gentiles, And their offspring among the people. All who see them shall

21) We confess on them, that at school/college/university they will find favour with their teachers/leaders and receive special attention for help. They will be selected for special programmes, public representation, scholarships, etc that will bring out their excellence in Jesus name.

22) We pray that they will progress and succeed at every stage of their development in life. They will pass all their exams, assessment or interviews in flying colours, in Jesus name.

*Isaiah 54:13 "All your children shall be taught
by the LORD, And great shall be the peace of
your children."*

23) We command gates of elevation and doors of divine acceptance to be open unto our children and youths, to receive the treasures of darkness and hidden riches of secret places, in Jesus name.

*Isaiah 60:11 "Therefore your gates shall be
open continually; They shall not be shut day or
night, That men may bring to you the wealth of
the Gentiles, And their kings in procession."*

24) Oh Lord release unto our children and youths, their destiny angels, guarding angels and ministering angels always in Jesus name.

Matthew 18:10 "Take heed that you do not despise one of these little ones, for I say to you that in heaven their angels always see the face of My Father who is in heaven."

Hebrew 1:14 "Are they not all ministering spirits sent forth to minister for those who will inherit salvation Psalm 34:7; The angel of the LORD encamps all around those who fear Him And delivers them."

<u>CONSISTENT DECLARATION ON CHILDREN</u>

My children are taught of the Lord and great is their peace.

My children shall know the Lord, serve the Lord, love the Lord, obey the Lord, fear the Lord and trust the Lord.

My children are well behaved, obedient and good citizens.

My children's steps are ordered by the Lord.

My children will live right, go to the right schools, get in the right career, profession or business.

My children will grow and become strong in the spirit.

My children will increase in wisdom and stature.

My children are anointed with Oil of favour and they have favour before God and all men.

My children are for signs and wonders in the land of the living.

My children will live well, live godly and live long.

My children are God's Battle axe and weapon of war.

My children are Gods general and rescue squads.

My children are God chosen to occupy till Jesus comes.

My children are not vagabond, wanderers or outcast.

My children are not weak, helpless, hopeless or powerless.

My children are the hope of tomorrow.

My children will not abandon me, forget me or hate me.

My children will go from glory to glory, strength to strength, and honour to honour.

My children will sit with kings and princes.

My children's gifts, talents, potentials and divine assignments will make room for them.

My children will excel, succeed, and make me proud.

My children are always blessed and highly favoured.

My children will do great exploits, and break limits.

My children will be agents of change.

My children will conquer territories.

My children will be overcomers.

Wrong friends will not ruin the lives of my children

Wrong association will not bury the glory of my children

My children are disconnected from wrong people and connected to the right people.

My children will be the Joseph and Esther of the family.

My children will become Global Ambassador and International Icon.

TURNAROUND CHALLENGES ON CHILDREN

My children will not bring me shame or disgrace.

My children will not suffer infirmities and affliction.

My children will not suffer for another person's error.

My children will not be victims of accident, abuse, racism, bullying or rape.

My children will come back from the land of the enemy, and back to their own borders. *(Jeremiah 31:16-17)*

My children are coming back to their original, out of every vice, sorcery and bewitchment. *(Acts 8:9-11)*

My children will be delivered and restored, out of every snares, traps, and prisons. *(Isaiah 42:22)*

My children's eye gate, ear gate, and mind gate will open, to hear the word of God and be converted and healed. *(Acts 28:26-27)*

My children's soul is escaped as a bird out of the snare of the fowler. *(Psalm 124:7)*

My children is delivered from the power of darkness and translated into the kingdom of God's dear Son. *(Colossians 1:13)*

My children are redeemed by the Blood of Jesus, and receive forgiveness of sins. *(Colossians 1:14)*

My children will not follow the voice of strangers. *(John 10:5)*

My children will be delivered from the hand of strange children. *(Psalm 144:7)*

My children's soul is loosed from prison of wrong expectations, judgement and curses. (Psalm 142:7)

I break my children free from ungodly soul ties and pray for godly soul ties that will bring them blessings.

I will not labour in vain nor bring forth children for trouble; they are the offspring of the blessed of the Lord. *(Isaiah 65:23a)*

I will not build and another inhabit, I will not plant and another eat, I will not sow and another reap; *(Isaiah 65:22)*

I will enjoy the fruit of my labour over my children. *(Isaiah 65:23b)*

My God is my refuge and strength, He will help me through all troubles; He will cover my head in the day of battle. *(Psalm 46:1; Psalm 140:7)*

Please combine all Prayers for Children and Young people above with this section *

HEALING SCRIPTURES DECLARATIONS ON CHILDREN

(To deal with Physical, Emotional, Spiritual, Mental, Financial, Marital/Marriage Problems)

I command Supernatural healing power to enter my child/children now, to flow from the top of their head to the soles of their feet now in Jesus name.

I rebuke that health problem (name it.... mental/emotional /physical....) in my child/children's life in Jesus name.

I command Light in the Darkness of this Health situation in Jesus name. I stand on, Psalm 27:1-2

> *"The Lord is my light and my salvation; whom shall I fear? the Lord is the strength of my life; of whom shall I be afraid? When the wicked, even mine enemies and my foes, came upon me to eat up my flesh, they stumbled and fell."*

Oh Great Physician, you are my light & salvation by all the power for which you are known to be God, arise and give my child/children total healing from this affliction / sickness / infirmity in the name of Jesus.

I declare my child/children's healing now in Jesus name. I infuse my child/children's life with the power of God through His Word:

Isaiah 53:5;

> *"But he was wounded for our transgressions, he was bruised for our iniquities: the chastisement of our peace was upon him; and with his stripes we are healed."*

Psalm 103:3;

> *"Who forgiveth all thine iniquities; who healeth all thy diseases; Who redeemeth thy life from destruction; who crowneth thee with lovingkindness and tender mercies;"*

Psalm 107:20;

> *"He sent his word, and healed them, and delivered them from their destructions."*

Matt 8:16-17;

> *"When the even was come, they brought unto him many that were possessed with devils: and he cast out the spirits with his word, and healed all that were sick: That it might be fulfilled which was spoken by Esaias the prophet, saying, Himself took our infirmities, and bare our sicknesses."*

1 Peter 2:24;

> *"Who his own self bare our sins in his own body on the tree, that we, being dead to sins, should live unto righteousness: by whose stripes ye were healed."*

Proverbs 4:20-22;

> *"My son, attend to my words; incline thine ear unto my sayings. Let them not depart from thine eyes; keep them in the midst of thine heart. For they are life unto those that find them, and health to all their flesh."*

1 John 3:8;

> *"He that committeth sin is of the devil; for the devil sinneth from the beginning. For this purpose the Son of God was manifested, that he might destroy the works of the devil."*

Malachi 4:2-3;

> *"But unto you that fear my name shall the Sun of righteousness arise with healing in his wings; and ye shall go forth, and grow up as calves of the stall. And ye shall tread down the wicked; for they shall be ashes under the soles of your feet in the day that I shall do this, saith the Lord of hosts"*

Exodus 15:26;

> *"And said, If thou wilt diligently hearken to the
> voice of the Lord thy God, and wilt do that
> which is right in his sight, and wilt give ear to
> his commandments, and keep all his statutes, I
> will put none of these diseases upon thee,
> which I have brought upon the Egyptians: for I
> am the Lord that healeth thee."*

Exodus 23:25;

> *"And ye shall serve the Lord your God, and he
> shall bless thy bread, and thy water; and I will
> take sickness away from the midst of thee."*

Jeremiah 30:17 ;

> *"For I will restore health unto thee, and I will
> heal thee of thy wounds, saith the Lord;
> because they called thee an Outcast, saying,
> This is Zion, whom no man seeketh after."*

Luke 8:43-44;

> *"And a woman having an issue of blood twelve
> years, which had spent all her living upon
> physicians, neither could be healed of any,
> Came behind him, and touched the border of
> his garment: and immediately her issue of
> blood stanched."*

3 John 1:2;

> *"Beloved, I wish above all things that thou mayest prosper and be in health, even as thy soul prospereth."*

Luke 6:18-19;

> *"And they that were vexed with unclean spirits: and they were healed. And the whole multitude sought to touch him: for there went virtue out of him, and healed them all."*

Psalm 91:1-16;

> *"He that dwelleth in the secret place of the most High shall abide under the shadow of the Almighty. I will say of the Lord, He is my refuge and my fortress: my God; in him will I trust. Surely he shall deliver thee from the snare of the fowler, and from the noisome pestilence. He shall cover thee with his feathers, and under his wings shalt thou trust: his truth shall be thy shield and buckler. Thou shalt not be afraid for the terror by night; nor for the arrow that flieth by day; Nor for the pestilence that walketh in darkness; nor for the destruction that wasteth at noonday. A thousand shall fall at thy side, and ten thousand at thy right hand; but it shall not come nigh thee. Only with thine eyes shalt thou behold*

and see the reward of the wicked.... Because thou hast made the Lord, which is my refuge, even the most High, thy habitation; There shall no evil befall thee, neither shall any plague come nigh thy dwelling. For he shall give his angels charge over thee, to keep thee in all thy ways. They shall bear thee up in their hands, lest thou dash thy foot against a stone. Thou shalt tread upon the lion and adder: the young lion and the dragon shalt thou trample under feet. Because he hath set his love upon me, therefore will I deliver him: I will set him on high, because he hath known my name. He shall call upon me, and I will answer him: I will be with him in trouble; I will deliver him, and honour him. With long life will I satisfy him, and shew him my salvation."

Oh Lord send your Angels - the heavenly doctors & nurses to perform your divine surgical operation on my child/children and apply the oil of the balm of Gilead all over my child/children in Jesus name. Amen.

James 5:14-15:

"Is any sick among you? let him call for the elders of the church; and let them pray over him, anointing him with oil in the name of the Lord: And the prayer of faith shall save the sick, and the Lord shall raise him up; and if he

*have committed sins, they shall be forgiven
him."*

-All sickness and infirmities planted in my child/children's
life be uprooted now, and go back to sender in Jesus name.'
Amen.

-We release your power in the blood of Jesus and Fire of
the Holy Ghost to flow and flush out every seed of infirmity
now in Jesus name.

Matthew18:18-19:

*"Verily I say unto you, Whatsoever ye shall
bind on earth shall be bound in heaven: and
whatsoever ye shall loose on earth shall be
loosed in heaven. Again I say unto you, That if
two of you shall agree on earth as touching any
thing that they shall ask, it shall be done for
them of my Father which is in heaven."*

-We bind you spirit of infirmity in Jesus name, We
command you to leave my child/children's body now in
Jesus name. You demonic spirits of sickness & diseases,
We curse you to the roots, we command you to die now in
Jesus name. Be bound and get out of my child/children's
body now in Jesus name.

It is written in 2 Timothy 4:18

*"And the Lord shall deliver me from every evil
work, and will preserve me unto his heavenly*

*kingdom: to whom be glory for ever and ever.
Amen."*

-I declare my child/children's complete healing and deliverance now, by the Anointing the yoke of sickness is broken forever and my child/children walk in victory and freedom to live a prosperous life and will run the race successfully to make heaven in Jesus name. Amen.

Chapter Three

WARFARE DECLARATIONS

I Declare warfare scriptures to contend in battle against powers and evil spirits warring against my life, assigned to cause:

- Hurts & pains;

- Sicknesses, diseases & afflictions;

- Oppression, bondage & imprisonments;

- Poverty & lack of anything;

- Troubled situations;

- Curses, Evil tongues, evil speakers;

- Hindrances & blockages;

- Closed gates/doors, demonic gatekeepers;

- Impending danger or destruction;

- Especially evil dreams;

I say no, you will not prosper in my life, in Jesus name.

I renounce every satanic & demonic activities, evil altars, covenants, and sacrifices that gave you access into my life;

I renounce it,

I reject it,

I cancel it

I destroy it

I break your power over my life, in Jesus name.

The Word of God is Fire, it is a hammer that breaks the rocks in pieces, and it is Sword in the Spirit.

As I declare the Word, I command it to go forth and locate all the powers and spirits, to break them into pieces in Jesus name.

I declare:

Psalm 27:1-2:

"The Lord is my light and my salvation; whom shall I fear? The Lord is the strength of my life; of whom shall I be afraid? When the wicked, even mine enemies and my foes, came upon me to eat up my flesh, they stumbled and fell."

Ephesians 6:10-18

"Finally, my brethren, be strong in the Lord, and in the power of his might. Put on the whole armour of God, that ye may be able to stand against the wiles of the devil. For we wrestle not against flesh and blood, but against principalities, against powers, against the rulers of the darkness of this world, against spiritual wickedness in high places. Wherefore take unto you the whole armour of God, that ye may be able to withstand in the evil day, and having done all, to stand. Stand therefore, having your loins girt about with truth, and having on the breastplate of righteousness; And

your feet shod with the preparation of the gospel of peace; Above all, taking the shield of faith, wherewith ye shall be able to quench all the fiery darts of the wicked. And take the helmet of salvation, and the sword of the Spirit, which is the word of God: Praying always with all prayer and supplication in the Spirit, and watching thereunto with all perseverance and supplication for all saints;"

Obadiah 1:17-18

"But upon mount Zion shall be deliverance, and there shall be holiness; and the house of Jacob shall possess their possessions. And the house of Jacob shall be a fire, and the house of Joseph a flame, and the house of Esau for stubble, and they shall kindle in them, and devour them; and there shall not be any remaining of the house of Esau; for the Lord hath spoken it."

Isaiah49:24-26

"Shall the prey be taken from the mighty, or the lawful captive delivered? But thus saith the Lord, Even the captives of the mighty shall be taken away, and the prey of the terrible shall be delivered: for I will contend with him that contendeth with thee, and I will save thy children. And I will feed them that oppress

thee with their own flesh; and they shall be drunken with their own blood, as with sweet wine: and all flesh shall know that I the Lord am thy Saviour and thy Redeemer, the mighty One of Jacob."

Luke 10:19

"Behold, I give unto you power to tread on serpents and scorpions, and over all the power of the enemy: and nothing shall by any means hurt you.

Isaiah 25:7-8

"And he will destroy in this mountain the face of the covering cast over all people, and the veil that is spread over all nations. He will swallow up death in victory; and the Lord God will wipe away tears from off all faces; and the rebuke of his people shall he take away from off all the earth: for the Lord hath spoken it."

Jeremiah 1:10

"See, I have this day set thee over the nations and over the kingdoms, to root out, and to pull down, and to destroy, and to throw down, to build, and to plant."

Colossians 2:14-15

"Blotting out the handwriting of ordinances that was against us, which was contrary to us, and took it out of the way, nailing it to his cross; And having spoiled principalities and powers, he made a shew of them openly, triumphing over them in it."

Isaiah 22:25

"In that day, saith the Lord of hosts, shall the nail that is fastened in the sure place be removed, and be cut down, and fall; and the burden that was upon it shall be cut off: for the Lord hath spoken it.

Ezekiel 38:22

"And I will bring him to judgment with pestilence and bloodshed; I will rain down on him, on his troops, and on the many peoples who are with him, flooding rain, great hailstones, fire, and brimstone."

Malachi 4:2-3

"But unto you that fear my name shall the Sun of righteousness arise with healing in his wings; and ye shall go forth, and grow up as calves of the stall. And ye shall tread down the wicked; for they shall be ashes under the soles of your feet in the day that I shall do this, saith the Lord of hosts."

Psalm 18:28-29

"For thou wilt light my candle: the Lord my God will enlighten my darkness. For by thee I have run through a troop; and by my God have I leaped over a wall."

Romans 8:28-31

"And we know that all things work together for good to them that love God, to them who are the called according to his purpose. For whom he did foreknow, he also did predestinate to be conformed to the image of his Son, that he might be the firstborn among many brethren. Moreover whom he did predestinate, them he also called: and whom he called, them he also justified: and whom he justified, them he also glorified. What shall we then say to these things? If God be for us, who can be against us?"

Deuteronomy 33:27

"The eternal God is thy refuge, and underneath are the everlasting arms: and he shall thrust out the enemy from before thee; and shall say, Destroy them."

Jeremiah 20:11

"But the Lord is with me as a mighty terrible one: therefore my persecutors shall stumble, and they shall not prevail: they shall be greatly ashamed; for they shall not prosper: their everlasting confusion shall never be forgotten."

Ezekiel 34:25-28

"And I will make with them a covenant of peace, and will cause the evil beasts to cease out of the land: and they shall dwell safely in the wilderness, and sleep in the woods. And I will make them and the places round about my hill a blessing; and I will cause the shower to come down in his season; there shall be showers of blessing. And the tree of the field shall yield her fruit, and the earth shall yield her increase, and they shall be safe in their land, and shall know that I am the Lord, when I have broken the bands of their yoke, and delivered them out of the hand of those that served themselves of them. And they shall no more be a prey to the heathen, neither shall the beast of the land devour them; but they shall dwell safely, and none shall make them afraid."

Isaiah 45:1-3

"Thus saith the Lord to his anointed, to Cyrus, whose right hand I have holden, to subdue nations before him; and I will loose the loins of kings, to open before him the two leaved gates; and the gates shall not be shut; I will go before thee, and make the crooked places straight: I will break in pieces the gates of brass, and cut in sunder the bars of iron: And I will give thee the treasures of darkness, and hidden riches of secret places, that thou mayest know that I, the Lord, which call thee by thy name, am the God of Israel."

Jeremiah 51:20-25,53

"Thou art my battle axe and weapons of war: for with thee will I break in pieces the nations, and with thee will I destroy kingdoms; and with thee will I break in pieces the horse and his rider; and with thee will I break in pieces the chariot and his rider; with thee also will I break in pieces man and woman; and with thee will I break in pieces old and young; and with thee will I break in pieces the young man and the maid; I will also break in pieces with thee the shepherd and his flock; and with thee will I break in pieces the husbandman and his yoke of oxen; and with thee will I break in pieces captains and rulers. And I will render unto

Babylon and to all the inhabitants of Chaldea all their evil that they have done in Zion in your sight, saith the LORD. Behold, I am against thee, O destroying mountain, saith the LORD, which destroyest all the earth: and I will stretch out mine hand upon thee, and roll thee down from the rocks, and will make thee a burnt mountain. Though Babylon should mount up to heaven, and though she should fortify the height of her strength, yet from me shall spoilers come unto her, saith the LORD."

Note: *Always engage the above warfare scriptures before you go into deliverance prayers and ministrations, or major spiritual warfare sessions.*

OTHER BOOKS BY THE AUTHOR:

Triumph over Satan

Mighty in Battle

Spiritual Warfare with the Blood of Jesus

From Barrenness to Fruitfulness – Spiritual Warfare

Woman Trim Your Lamp